LISTEN & OBEY

HEARING GOD'S VOICE

Listen & Obey: Hearing God's Voice

Devoted: Discipleship Training for Small Groups

Copyright © 2019 by Clear Creek Community Church and Ryan Lehtinen, Yancey Arrington, and Bruce Wesley

Editorial Team: Mandy Turner, Ryan Lehtinen, Jon Coffey

Published by Clear Creek Resources

A Ministry of Clear Creek Community Church

999 North FM 270

League City, Texas 77573

ISBN-13: 978-0-9979469-3-2

Unless otherwise indicated, all Scripture quotations are taken from:

The Holy Bible: English Standard Version, copyright © 2001 by Crossway Bibles, a division of Good News Publishers. Used by permission. All rights reserved.

All Scripture emphases have been added by the authors.

Printed in the United States of America

CONTENTS

INTRODUCTION

What if you could hear God's voice?

This study is designed to train you to be a citizen who, because you've been called by the king, listens to and obeys the voice of God.

Since its founding, Clear Creek Community Church has had one mission: to lead unchurched people to become fully devoted followers of Jesus Christ. This mission is simply a modern restating of Jesus' words in Matthew 28:19-20 where he commissioned his followers to "make disciples" of the world around them. In essence, Christ shows us what a Christian is to be — a disciple who makes disciples. This is the purpose behind the Devoted: Discipleship Training for Small Groups series.

Hopefully by now you're becoming familiar with Spiritual Growth Grid and the three main storylines.

	REPENT & BELIEVE		
WHO GOD IS (Identity)	**WHAT GOD DID** (Activity)	**WHO WE ARE** (Identity)	**WHAT WE DO** (Activity)
KING	CALLED	CITIZENS	LISTEN & OBEY
FATHER	ADOPTED	FAMILY	LOVE & SERVE
SAVIOR	SENT	MISSIONARIES	GO & MULTIPLY

This study is part of the Listen & Obey storyline. Our aim over the next 12 weeks will be to equip you to hear God's voice in the various ways he communicates to his people. You will be trained to read and study the Bible. You will have opportunities to grow in your prayer life. And you will learn some tools to help you discern if you're hearing God correctly.

Believe it or not, Hearing God's Voice really is possible.

Let's get started.

Grace to you,
The Elders of Clear Creek Community Church

USING THE STUDY

Devoted is a two-year small group study series focused on training in the essentials of being a disciple who makes disciples. It is designed to help small groups grow deeper in the concepts of the Spiritual Growth Grid. This means, regardless of where you are on the spiritual journey, you play your part in the group each week when you:

Step 1: Memorize the Scripture

Throughout the study you will memorize key Bible passages specifically chosen for the topic. Practice reciting these each day. Try to fill in the blank spaces from memory as you prepare to recite the passages at your next small group meeting.

Step 2: Study the Scripture

The Bible passages are chosen because of the study's general theme. They are good Scriptures to know as either citizens, family, or missionaries. They don't necessarily relate directly to the day's teaching. This is a section where we want disciples to grow in the skill of observing and interpreting a text. The teaching that follows will deal with biblical application.

Step 3: Read the Teaching

Take your time to read through the day's teaching. The questions that follow are designed to help you better process the lesson in light of the Spiritual Growth Grid and apply the principles. Afterwards, take time to pray using the prompts provided.

Step 4: Do the Weekly Exercise

You will find a weekly exercise at the end of each week's Day 3 material. The exercises often employ different learning styles to practice the principles been taught. Be sure to not only do the exercise but the reflection section as well. The exercises are intended to help build your skill set as a disciple-making disciple.

Step 5: Ready Yourself for Group

The last section of each week's material concludes with the *Get Ready for Group* section. This allows you to summarize your key takeaways for the week in preparation for small group discussion. Please be sure to answer the final question concerning how the week's lessons help you better integrate the Spiritual Growth Grid. This will help your Navigator identify possible areas of further study in order to better live out one's gospel identity. Remember, the point is to be trained to be a disciple who makes disciples!

01

THE GOD WHO SPEAKS

SCRIPTURE MEMORY

Blessed is the man who walks not in the counsel of the wicked, nor stands in the way of sinners, nor sits in the seat of scoffers; but his delight is in the law of the Lord, and on his law he meditates day and night.

–Psalm 1:1-2

OUT OF DARKNESS GOD SPEAKS

Scripture Study

Genesis 1:1-3

In the beginning, God created the heavens and the earth. ² The earth was without form and void, and darkness was over the face of the deep. And the Spirit of God was hovering over the face of the waters. ³ And God said, "Let there be light," and there was light.

Observing the Text

What actions are taking place in this passage? Who is carrying out those actions?

____

____

____

How is the eaerth described?

____

____

____

Interpreting the Text

What is the overall feeling of the scene? How would you describe it visually?

____

____

____

What contrasts are present between verses 2 and 3?

____

____

____

Teaching

The greatest movies, stories, and books all begin with a dramatic, atten-tion-getting introduction, drawing you in from the very first scene. There is something so finely crafted, so confounding, so beautiful, so emotional, that you have to find out what happens in the rest of the story. You're hooked.

The Bible begins with this kind of introduction. Perhaps you have heard or read it so many times that its dramatic effect seems to have been lost. But try to imagine the impact of reading those opening lines for the first time. The story of the Bible starts like this:

> *In the beginning, God created the heavens and the earth. The earth was without form and void, and darkness was over the face of the deep. And the Spirit of God was hovering over the face of the waters.*
>
> Genesis 1:1-2

The Bible opens with God Almighty presiding over his formless and empty creation. There is darkness. There is the dreadful and mysterious waters. And there is a dramatic silence.

And God said, "Let there be light," and there was light.

Genesis 1:3

Out of the darkness and deafening silence God speaks. By his spoken word there is light, and not only light, but in the following verses the sun and stars, land and sea, even plants and animals of every kind come into existence by the word spoken from God. He commands that they exist and they exist. The entire universe is created out of nothing by the voice of God.

One of the most important truths we learn in the opening verses of the Bible is that God is all-powerful and all-knowing beyond comprehension — and yet is knowable. In both the method and result of his creative work, the Father establishes a pattern of revelation: he speaks so that his creation might hear; he creates light so that his creation might see. He desires for us to know him and have a relationship with him. Imagine that. The Almighty Creator who spoke the universe into existence is not only actively involved in the affairs of creation but also personally involved with the people he created. He not only knows you but has made himself known to you.

God didn't stop speaking when his creation was complete. The Bible itself is God's word throughout history recorded for us in various forms. In the Old Testament, God spoke to his people by inspiring human spokesmen or prophets who would speak and write what God wanted said. God used a variety of people to speak in a variety of ways. He used narrative, law, poetry, prophesy, and wisdom. Some parts are easier to understand than others, but the point is this: God speaks. The Bible is the story of how by his Word he created the world, and by his Word he will redeem and restore the world.

Are you hooked? The rest of the Bible is the story of God graciously pursuing a personal relationship with his people. Over the next twelve weeks, this study will equip you to hear God's voice as you deepen your personal relationship with him.

Questions for Reflection

Do you see God as someone who desires to be known or as hidden and incomprehensible? How might each perspective shape our study of God in his word?

____

____

____

How does God's creation of humanity intersect with his authority over it? In what ways does our culture's dismissal of divine creation lead to a dismissal of his rule? Why does this matter?

____

____

____

What steps can you take today to reawaken your wonder about our Creator's willingness to reveal himself to us? How would a rekindled awe change your approach to the spiritual disciplines?

____

____

____

Prayer

Thank God for his work in both creating the world and revealing himself to his creation. Pray that we would have eyes to see his work and ears to hear his word as we pursue the relationship he offers.

SCRIPTURE MEMORY

_______ is the man who walks not in the counsel of the wicked, nor stands in the way of sinners, nor sits in the seat of scoffers; but his________is in the law of the Lord, and on his law he meditates day and night.

–*Psalm 1:1-2*

UNDER THE RULE OF GOD

Scripture Study

Hebrews 1:1-2

Long ago, at many times and in many ways, God spoke to our fathers by the prophets, ² but in these last days he has spoken to us by his Son, whom he appointed the heir of all things, through whom also he created the world.

Observing the text

Who are the "fathers" in verse 1? What method did God use to speak to them?

____

____

____

In verse 2, how has God's way of speaking shifted?

____

____

____

Interpreting the text

Underline all the verbs in Hebrews 1:1-2. What connections do you see between activity and authority?

____

____

____

What does this passage show us about Jesus' identity?

____

____

____

Teaching

All children have a period in their lives when they assert their will. First-time parents are often shocked to find that their sweet little baby has turned into a defiant two-year-old, but this transformation is a normal part of child development. When children refuse to obey, it is a declaration that they are a human being and a free moral agent. They have a will to assert. This period, often referred to as the "terrible twos," begins when they are about eighteen months old and lasts, on average, about seventy-eight years.

The first storyline in the Spiritual Growth Grid is *Listen & Obey.* God is our king who has called us through the cross to be citizens who listen and obey. The problem is, as human beings, we don't like being told we need to obey. Something about the word "obey" may even cause us to recoil. This feeling is rooted in our desire for control.

We like to be the one who calls the shots. We want to determine how our money is spent. We want to choose how we use our time. This is a natural human tendency, but perhaps it's made worse by our cultural context. Our Western, individualistic worldview gives us the illusion that we're in control of everything around us, and that we're actually pretty good at being in control.

But a critical look at your track record of "being in control" probably shows that your control hasn't accomplished as much as you'd like to think. Even if you might feel good about the overall results you have achieved, you can also point to events or seasons in life when maintaining control didn't go so well. When we try to control everything, our lives spin out of control. Think about the biggest struggles you are facing right now. It could be a financial struggle, a relationship struggle, an addiction, or anything else. Isn't it true that putting ourselves in the place of God is at the heart of most of our struggles?

In the opening verses of Hebrews, we see God as the one in control. He spoke by the prophets. He has spoken by Jesus. He appointed Jesus to be the heir of all things. He created the world. God is in control, and his plan, all along, has been for us to live under his control. So God speaks to us, giving commands, rules, guidance, and our assignment is to Listen & Obey. This might be the simplest expression of a life of faith. Just listen to God and obey what he says. God equips us with wisdom, the divine perspective, and the knowledge of the right thing to do.

Throughout the Bible, God reveals who he is. From beginning to end, it is made clear that God is the ultimate leader, the sovereign authority of the universe who has the final say. God is King, and through the cross of Jesus Christ he has called you to be a citizen of his kingdom. Citizens Listen & Obey when their king speaks.

When we defy his leadership, we are effectively attempting to be our own king. We don't like what God says, so we try to take control, which always results in a life that is out of control. What happens next is of critical importance in your spiritual growth. Will you keep a white-knuckle grip on things you cannot control, or will you surrender control to your King?

This is what it means to repent and believe: Recognizing your attempts to be in control or the ways in which your life is already spinning out of control, turning back to Jesus, and surrendering control to him. When that happens, things are properly under the rule of God.

Are you in control, out of control, or under God's control? A life of repentance and belief looks like rearranging your life around his reign, deciding in advance that his way is the best way and that his words lead to life. When he speaks, you submit to his kingship and humbly follow.

Questions for Reflection

Think about the most pressing challenges in your life. Are each of these areas in your control, spinning out of control, or under God's control?

____

____

____

How have you seen your life spin out of control when you have failed to listen and obey?

____

____

____

In what ways do you need to repent of a desire to rule over your own life? How have you struggled to believe that God is a benevolent king and yield to his reign?

____

____

____

Prayer

Pray that Christ would turn your heart to base your relationship with him on continually responding to him with faith and repentance. Thank him for making that relationship possible through his death on the cross.

SCRIPTURE MEMORY

Blessed is the man who______not in the counsel of the_______, nor stands in the way of sinners, nor sits in the seat of scoffers; but his delight is in the____of the Lord, and on his law he meditates day and night.

–Psalm 1:1-2

JESUS AS THE WORD OF GOD

Scripture Study

Hebrews 1:1-2

Long ago, at many times and in many ways, God spoke to our fathers by the prophets, ² but in these last days he has spoken to us by his Son, whom he appointed the heir of all things, through whom also he created the world. ³ He is the radiance of the glory of God and the exact imprint of his nature, and he upholds the universe by the word of his power...

Observing the Text

The writer of Hebrews contrasts two different periods of time. What phrases does he use for each? To what time period does each of those phrases refer?

____

____

____

How did God speak in each time period?

____

____

____

What three things are said about Jesus in verse 2?

____

____

____

Interpreting the Text

How is Jesus different from how God spoke in the Old Testament?

____

____

____

Explain how Jesus is the fulfillment of how God spoke in the Old Testament.

____

____

____

Teaching

Have you ever wanted to hear God's voice? In a moment of desperation, have you ever begged God to reveal his presence by speaking clearly? If God really does speak to people, wouldn't it be nice to be one of those people who get to hear his voice? It would put to rest those moments of doubt that he exists or cares. Sometimes we feel that if God would just speak, we could know for sure. Here is the amazing truth of the Bible: *God has spoken to us by his Son.*

We wish God would speak audibly for us to hear, maybe telling us something new and exciting or giving us specific guidance on a major life decision. But Hebrews 1 tells us there is nothing better or more exciting than the fact that God has spoken to us through the person and work of Jesus Christ. In the Old Testament, God spoke through divinely inspired prophets. Out of love for his people, he communicated to them through these spokesmen, sent by God to carry his word to his people. The writer of Hebrews declares that in sending his Son, God was sending his Word directly to his people. Jesus is the ultimate revelation of God. His sinless life, death on the cross, resurrection from the grave, and ascension into heaven — all of it — is God's love-motivated communication to you.

The rest of the book of Hebrews shows that Jesus is better than the prophets, better than Moses, better than the temple, better than human priests. He is divine. He is God's Word in human flesh sent to rescue his people from sin and death.

It is easy for us to get wrapped up in our day-to-day worries and questions. They can seem to be the most pressing things in our lives. If God would just tell us what to do in specific situations, we would be much less anxious. Life would be easier if God was like a Magic 8-Ball. "God, should I take this job?" *It is decidedly so.* "Should I marry this person?" *Outlook not so good.*

God certainly cares about the day-to-day questions and concerns of his people. He invites you to come to him with all things, seek his wisdom and guidance, and obey in faith. But in Jesus, God has given you something better than yes-or-no answers to life's questions: a relationship with him. By faith in Jesus, God washes you clean from your sin, redeems you from bondage, and promises eternal life with him. Could God say anything better than that to you? Is there an answer from God that would lay your worries and questions to rest more than the person and work of Jesus? If you want to hear God speak, remember that he already has and still does today. Look to Jesus, his ultimate revelation. You might not always get the specific answer you are looking for, but God has given you the ultimate answer that you truly need.

Questions for Reflection

What are the most pressing concerns that have consumed your thoughts and prayers this week?

____

____

____

How can knowing that Jesus is God's ultimate revelation affect your day-to-day concerns and questions?

____

____

____

What truths do you need to believe more deeply about God in order to trust him with your concerns?

____

____

____

Prayer

Pray that God would show you any ways in which you need to repent of desiring a response more than a relationship. Ask him to strengthen your faith in the midst of difficulty, and thank him for revealing himself in the person of Jesus.

WEEKLY EXERCISE

BEGIN A JOURNAL

Journaling is a great tool to reflect on scripture and to express and submit any thoughts or emotions to God. It is a personalized way to reflect on what God is teaching you, with the aim of pressing it deeper into your heart. Journaling looks different for each person. For some, journaling is a creative process consisting of drawings and doodles. For others, it is merely writing a few key points of application on a passage that they read.

Your exercise this week is to get a journal and start using it. Read Colossians 1:15-20 and journal about what stands out to you. Try a few different approaches to discover what works best for you. Here are some suggestions to guide what you journal about:

- New insights you gain from a Bible passage
- Personal application — a goal for change and a plan for growth
- Conviction regarding sin
- Reflection on a recent event
- Prayer about a life concern
- Answers to your prayers
- Stories of how you've seen God at work

Get Ready for Group

Write your memorized Scripture.

What observations and interpretations of Scripture were most meaningful to you?

Summarize your key takeaway(s) for this week.

What will you tell the group about the results of your exercise this week?

How has this week helped you better understand and apply the Spiritual Growth Grid?

02

HOW GOD SPEAKS

SCRIPTURE MEMORY

Blessed is the man who walks not in the counsel of the wicked, nor stands in the way of sinners, nor sits in the seat of scoffers; but his delight is in the law of the Lord, and on his law he meditates day and night.

–Psalm 1:1-2

THE ALL-KNOWING GOD

Scripture Study

1 Corinthians 15:1-11

Now I would remind you, brothers, of the gospel I preached to you, which you received, in which you stand, ² and by which you are being saved, if you hold fast to the word I preached to you — unless you believed in vain. ³ For I delivered to you as of first importance what I also received: that Christ died for our sins in accordance with the Scriptures, ⁴ that he was buried, that he was raised on the third day in accordance with the Scriptures, ⁵ and that he appeared to Cephas, then to the twelve. ⁶ Then he appeared to more than five hundred brothers at one time, most of whom are still alive, though some have fallen asleep. ⁷ Then he appeared to James, then to all the apostles. ⁸ Last of all, as to one untimely born, he appeared also to me. ⁹ For I am the least of the apostles, unworthy to be called an apostle, because I persecuted the church of God. ¹⁰ But by the grace of God I am what I am, and his grace toward me was not in vain. On the contrary, I worked harder than any of them, though it was not I, but the grace of God that is with me. ¹¹ Whether then it was I or they, so we preach and so you believed.

Observing the Text

What is the gospel that Paul preached to the Corinthians?

____

____

____

What three verbs does Paul use to describe the Corinthians' response to the gospel he preached?

____

____

____

Interpreting the Text

Why is salvation in verse 2 described as something that is ongoing rather than completed?

____

____

____

Why is it significant that Paul adds the condition "if you hold fast to the word I preached to you"?

____

____

____

Teaching

The diversity of industries and businesses in Houston (and specifically the Bay Area) means there is an abundance of interesting and exciting professions. During Career Week at my (Ryan) daughter's elementary school, the students had an assembly in the gymnasium where they got to hear from an astronaut...while he was in space!

Projected on a large screen, the astronaut floated around the International Space Station while students from each grade had the opportunity to ask questions. My daughter was one of the selected students, so I went to watch her stand in line behind a microphone with about twenty other students. There were a lot of questions about going to the bathroom, which cleared some things up for me if I'm honest.

The astronaut answered each question thoroughly, providing interesting details while avoiding overly complicated technical language. If he had been giving a lecture to other space industry professionals, I'm sure he would have used different vocabulary (and would have to field fewer bathroom questions). But for the elementary school, his awareness of the audience led him to speak in a way that they could understand. As a result, the kids were captivated. It didn't hurt that he would occasionally do a backflip, for no reason other than when you're in space you can.

In a similar way, God is very aware of his audience. His wisdom, knowledge, and power are limitless, yet he speaks in a way that humans can understand. The infinite God is communicating with finite humanity. This is an important concept to grasp when talking about hearing God's voice, especially as it relates to interpreting the Bible. As we study the Bible, we must acknowledge the accommodation of divine truths to human minds.

> *For my thoughts are not your thoughts, neither are your ways my ways, declares the Lord. For as the heavens are higher than the earth, so are my ways higher than your ways and my thoughts than your thoughts.*
>
> Isaiah 55:8-9

This truth has implications for how we hear from God. First, it should cause us to see God rightly, provoking awe and wonder. We must acknowledge the omniscience of God. The chasm between God's knowledge and ours is infinitely larger than that of the knowledge of an astronaut and an elementary school student. He knows everything from all eternity. The smartest scientist who can explain the most complex phenomena in nature is just a kindergartner with a magnifying glass compared to God's matchless wisdom. Any attempt to grasp the knowledge of God should lead us to worship.

Second, acknowledging God's accommodation to human understanding should cause us to see ourselves rightly before him. Reflecting on God's limitless knowledge will clearly expose the limits of our own. There is a level of humility that should naturally emerge when talking with someone whose knowledge on a topic surpasses our own. No one likes a know-it-all, because we know that no one really knows it all. How foolish would it be for elementary school students to try to present themselves as experts equally competent to an astronaut! We must drop the act and approach hearing God with an appropriate level of humility, aware that he knows more than we could possibly imagine.

Worship and humility are key components of hearing God's voice. By submitting ourselves to the authority of God's voice in our lives, we recognize how amazing it is that God would speak in ways that we can understand.

Questions for Reflection

What did you learn about God from today's teaching section?

____

____

____

What did you learn about yourself from today's teaching section?

____

____

____

How does recognizing God's infinite knowledge and our finite knowledge cause you to live differently?

____

____

____

Prayer

Praise God for his infinite, eternal, perfect knowledge, and that he chooses to reveal knowledge of himself to us. Pray that we would be filled with wonder and humility as we approach his word and listen for his voice.

SCRIPTURE MEMORY

Blessed is the man who walks_______

__________of the wicked, nor stands

in the way of sinners, nor sits_______

_____________; but his delight is in

the law of the Lord, and on his law

he meditates day and night.

–Psalm 1:1-2

HOW GOD SPEAKS TODAY

Scripture Study

1 Corinthians 15:1-11

Now I would remind you, brothers, of the gospel I preached to you, which you received, in which you stand, 2 and by which you are being saved, if you hold fast to the word I preached to you—unless you believed in vain. 3 For I delivered to you as of first importance what I also received: that Christ died for our sins in accordance with the Scriptures, 4 that he was buried, that he was raised on the third day in accordance with the Scriptures, 5 and that he appeared to Cephas, then to the twelve. 6 Then he appeared to more than five hundred brothers at one time, most of whom are still alive, though some have fallen asleep. 7 Then he appeared to James, then to all the apostles. 8 Last of all, as to one untimely born, he appeared also to me. 9 For I am the least of the apostles, unworthy to be called an apostle, because I persecuted the church of God. 10 But by the grace of God I am what I am, and his grace toward me was not in vain. On the contrary, I worked harder than any of them, though it was not I, but the grace of God that is with me. 11 Whether then it was I or they, so we preach and so you believed.

Observing the text

According to verses 3-5, how does Paul summarize the central message of the Christian faith?

____

____

____

To whom did Jesus appear after his resurrection?

____

____

____

Interpreting the text

Why does Paul emphasize that things happened "in accordance with the Scriptures"?

____

____

____

Why would it be significant that most of those to whom Jesus appeared after his resurrection are still alive at the time Paul wrote this letter?

____

____

____

Teaching

To hear God's voice, we must recognize that he speaks in a variety of ways. Because God has no limits, he is capable of speaking whenever and however he chooses. If God spoke through a donkey (Numbers 22:28) and a burning bush (Exodus 3:4), then surely he can still speak in extraordinary ways. However, the ways in which God ordinarily speaks to his people today can be divided up into the following broad categories, which we will discuss in more depth in the coming weeks.

God speaks through the Bible. The authoritative word of God is the primary way God speaks today. The voice of God is clearest in the Scriptures. It is through the Bible that we can study, evaluate, and interpret what God is saying. As Bruce often says, "When you open the Bible, God opens his mouth." Therefore, all other ways that God might speak today must be tested against what he says in the Bible. For example, if someone tells you, "God told me to leave my spouse for another person I've fallen in love with," we know that person has been deceived because this would contradict the Bible. They are not hearing God's voice in this matter. God will not contradict his word. Because Scripture is our final authority, we will spend the majority of this study learning how to study the Bible.

> *All Scripture is breathed out by God and profitable for teaching,*
> *for reproof, for correction, and for training in righteousness.*
>
> 2 Timothy 3:16

God speaks through the inner witness of the Holy Spirit. When Jesus was preparing his disciples for his departure, he encouraged them by telling them that the Holy Spirit would not only be with them when he was gone, but that the Holy Spirit would be in them. What an amazing thing!

> *And I will ask the Father, and he will give you another Helper,*
> *to be with you forever, even the Spirit of truth, whom the world*
> *cannot receive, because it neither sees him nor knows him. You*
> *know him, for he dwells with you and will be in you.*
>
> John 14:16-17

This means that we can hear from God through the inner witness of the Holy Spirit. Though he generally will not speak with an audible voice, we may hear the Holy Spirit as we read the Bible, as we pray, or through a kind of "prompting," which we might describe as an inner sense or confirmation. Spending regular time reading the Bible, praying, and engaging in other spiritual disciplines helps to tune our ears to hear the Holy Spirit speak in this way. As previously mentioned, it is critical to test any inner leading against scripture.

God speaks through external means. In his sovereignty, God will often speak to us through external means. Most commonly, this is through the wise counsel of other believers. When seeking to hear God's voice and discern his will, we ought to seek counsel from mature followers of Jesus who can help us test our thoughts and feelings against Scripture. Through their experience, knowledge, and the inner witness of the Holy Spirit, they can help us gain clarity about God's plan.

A less common, and often less reliable, way that we might hear God's voice is through circumstances. God is sovereign over everything, and therefore, it is conceivable that he orchestrates circumstances to make his will known to his children. However, attempting to interpret our circumstances in order to hear God's voice is often very unreliable. People might ask God to "open or close a door" as a sign of whether he wants them to do something or not. This kind of prayer is not necessarily wrong, but should not be the primary way to discern God's will. "Open doors" don't always mean we should move ahead. Likewise, "closed doors" don't always mean we should stop. Perhaps God wants to kick the door down in answer to your prayer! Therefore, wise counsel, prayer, and the Bible should be the normative ways we hear God's voice and discern his will.

The role of the Holy Spirit is crucial to hearing God's voice — whether through the Bible, his inner witness, or other external means. We must rely on his power and wisdom to know that it is God's voice we are hearing and not our own.

Questions for Reflection

Have you ever been certain that you heard God's voice? In what way did he speak? How were you sure that it was God who spoke?

____

____

____

Have you ever been in a situation where you really needed to hear God's voice but he didn't seem to speak to you? How did that experience make you feel?

____

____

____

How do you normally seek to hear God speak to you?

____

____

____

Prayer

Thank God for sending the Holy Spirit to help, comfort, and guide us through our daily decisions. Ask the Spirit to clearly lead as you seek to hear God's voice and do his will.

SCRIPTURE MEMORY

_______________________ who walks not in

the_____________________________, nor stands

in the way of sinners, nor sits in the

seat of scoffers; but his____________

_____________________, and on his law

he meditates day and night.

–Psalm 1:1-2

HEALTHY SKEPTICISM

Scripture Study

1 Corinthians 15:1-11

Now I would remind you, brothers, of the gospel I preached to you, which you received, in which you stand, [2] and by which you are being saved, if you hold fast to the word I preached to you — unless you believed in vain. [3] For I delivered to you as of first importance what I also received: that Christ died for our sins in accordance with the Scriptures, [4] that he was buried, that he was raised on the third day in accordance with the Scriptures, [5] and that he appeared to Cephas, then to the twelve. [6] Then he appeared to more than five hundred brothers at one time, most of whom are still alive, though some have fallen asleep. [7] Then he appeared to James, then to all the apostles. [8] Last of all, as to one untimely born, he appeared also to me. [9] For I am the least of the apostles, unworthy to be called an apostle, because I persecuted the church of God. [10] But by the grace of God I am what I am, and his grace toward me was not in vain. On the contrary, I worked harder than any of them, though it was not I, but the grace of God that is with me. [11] Whether then it was I or they, so we preach and so you believed.

Observing the Text

Why does Paul call himself unworthy of being called an apostle?

____

____

____

To whom does Paul attribute this hard work?

____

____

____

Interpreting the Text

What does Paul mean by "his grace toward me was not in vain"?

____

____

____

What's the connection between Paul's hard work and God's grace in accomplishing things for God's glory?

____

____

____

Teaching

Every year, the news is filled with headlines about a record-breaking lottery jackpot, sometimes totaling over $1 billion. Seeing all those zeros causes people to run out and get tickets, hoping to be that lucky winner. Then the fantasies begin. At work, at home, at the ball field, people ask each other, "What would you do with $1 billion?" The mansions, Lamborghinis, private jets, and yachts seem like they're already yours. With your stack of $50 in lottery tickets, it's a sure thing. What will you do the morning after you win? What are you going to say to your boss when you quit?

Of course, when the numbers are drawn, your stack of lottery tickets is worthless. What seemed certain turned out to be wrong. The fantasy that seemed so real in your mind turned out to be just your imagination. It was never real; it was never a sure thing. In reality, that particular drawing had a one in 302,575,350 chance of winning. But for a moment you believed it was going to happen.

Some people have a similar experience when trying to hear God's voice. Larry had a strong sense that God was telling him to quit his job and start a company in the oil industry. And not only would he start this company, he also felt certain that God had promised that this company would be financially successful. He thought to himself, *If God put this on my heart, it must be true.* With this divine guarantee of success, he quit his job, took out a second mortgage on his home, and started this new company.

Six months later, the company went bankrupt, and Larry lost everything. He had been convinced that God had promised a sure success, but it turned out to not be so sure. He was angry with God, wondering what happened to the promise in which he had placed all his hope.

Maybe Larry was misled by his own desires to run his own company and achieve financial success. It could be that Larry heard correctly that God was leading him to start this company, but he was mistaken that financial success was guaranteed. There was breakdown somewhere in Larry hearing God's voice. Was it God's voice he was hearing, or was it his own?

As we learn how to hear God's voice through the various means he uses to reveal his will, it's helpful for us to maintain a healthy skepticism towards ourselves. When God speaks, his voice is not the only voice we hear. Every day our culture, our family and friends, and our own desires compete for our attention. Sometimes those other voices speak louder in the ears of our heart, drowning out what God is saying to us. If we're honest, we may sometimes like what those other voices are saying more than what God is saying. But a citizen of God's kingdom seeks to listen to and obey no other voice than the voice of God.

Therefore, we approach God with a desire to hear his voice over the voice of others. This requires us to humbly admit we're prone to mistaking his voice for the voice of others, and to ask him to help us to discern his voice within the cacophony in our heads. Thankfully, God is patient with our natural limitations, and he speaks in a variety of ways. We can ask him to confirm what we believe he is saying to us while repenting of our tendency to let our desires control our path.

Questions for Reflection

Have you ever acted on something knowing it wasn't what God wanted for you but you did it anyway? How did that situation turn out?

____

____

____

What voices in your head do you listen to most often—God, culture, your desires, people, etc.?

____

____

____

Why do you listen and obey other voices in your head rather than God's?

____

____

____

Prayer

Praise our God who patiently speaks, lowering himself to reveal his will to his creatures who fail to listen and obey over and over again. Pray that we would recognize his voice as we grow in the habit of seeking to hear his voice.

WEEKLY EXERCISE

SELF-ASSESSMENT

Answer the following questions by circling the word that best describes you. This is not to judge your level of spirituality or compare yourself to others. There is no scoring involved. These questions should help you reflect on how you are living into the beliefs and practices you would like to have for yourself.

1. When I need direction and wisdom, my first impulse is to go to God by reading the Bible and praying.

   Never | Rarely | Sometimes | Often | Always

2. I set aside time during my day to read the Bible and pray.

   Never | Rarely | Sometimes | Often | Always

3. I am confused by what I read in the Bible.

   Never | Rarely | Sometimes | Often | Always

4. I know what to read in the Bible to discern God's will.

   Strongly Disagree | Disagree | Undecided | Agree | Strongly Agree

5. When I pray I sense the presence of the Holy Spirit.

   Never | Rarely | Sometimes | Often | Always

6. Prayer is an important and regular part of my life.

   Not at all | Slightly | Moderately | Very

7. I have at least one person in my life, who I would consider godly, that I go to for counsel.

   Strongly Disagree | Disagree | Undecided | Agree | Strongly Agree

8. When I sense that the Holy Spirit is leading me in a certain way I obey
what he says.
Never | Rarely | Sometimes | Often | Always

9. When I need to make a decision, I trust my gut which is usually right.
Strongly Disagree | Disagree | Undecided | Agree | Strongly Agree

10. I am confident that I am hearing God's voice in my life right now.
Strongly Disagree | Disagree | Undecided | Agree | Strongly Agree

Summarize your reflections from this exercise.

____

____

____

____

____

____

____

____

Get Ready for Group

Write your memorized Scripture.

____

____

____

____

____

What observations and interpretations of Scripture were most meaningful to you?

____

____

____

____

____

Summarize your key takeaway(s) for this week.

____

____

____

____

____

What will you tell the group about the results of your exercise this week?

____

____

____

____

____

How has this week helped you better understand and apply the Spiritual Growth Grid?

____

____

____

____

____

03

THE BIBLE AS THE WORD OF GOD

SCRIPTURE MEMORY

All Scripture is breathed out by God and profitable for teaching, for reproof, for correction, and for training in righteousness, that the man of God may be complete, equipped for every good work. –*2 Timothy 3:16-17*

THE BIBLE AS THE WORD OF GOD

Scripture Study

2 Timothy 3:16-17

All Scripture is breathed out by God and profitable for teaching, for reproof, for correction, and for training in righteousness, [17] that the man of God may be complete, equipped for every good work.

Observing the Text

What are some other places in the Bible where God breathes?

____

____

____

According to this passage, how is reading the Bible useful for a follower of Christ?

____

____

____

What is the end result of reading the Bible?

____

____

____

Interpreting the Text

What does it mean that Scripture is breathed out by God?

____

____

____

Why is it significant that the purpose of reading the Bible is not limited to gaining knowledge?

____

____

____

Teaching

There is a really good chance you own a Bible. In fact, there is a really good chance you own multiple Bibles. A recent survey found that 88 percent of Americans own a Bible, and those who own a Bible have on average 3.5 Bibles in their home.[1] This should come as no surprise — according to Guinness World Records, the Bible is the best-selling book of all time with over five billion copies sold and distributed.[2] Although it's very common for someone to have a Bible on their bookshelf or on their coffee table,

---

1 "What Do Americans Really Think About the Bible?" Barna Group, 2013, www.barna.com/research/what-do-americans-really-think-about-the-bible/#.V8WEbbX38VE.

2 "Best-Selling Book of Non-Fiction." Guinness World Records, www.guinnessworldrecords.com/world-records/best-selling-book-of-non-fiction/.

it's far less common for that Bible to be opened regularly. Only one in five Bible owners read the Bible four or more times a week. Why would that be?

David Kinnaman, President of Barna Group, explains the low percentage of regular Bible reading when he says, "Even if there's a baseline of respect, people aren't sure how to apply the lessons of Scripture to public life or society, particularly in an increasingly pluralistic nation."[3] The majority of Bibles collect dust on the bookshelf because most people don't know how to study and apply the Bible to their lives. Even when they've tried to read it, after a few minutes they set it down, confused and discouraged. Maybe you can relate. But with some training, effort, and an encouraging community, you can regularly engage the Bible in a way that is not only relevant but life-changing.

No matter how many Bibles you have, God's Word cannot be helpful until you open it, engage it, read it, study it, and most of all, apply it. That's what faith looks like: we hear God speak, trust who he is, and do what he says.

So, let's start with an overview. The Bible is a collection of sixty-six books written over a period of 1,500 years, on three different continents, in three different languages, by almost forty different human writers. Yet, the storyline of each of those individual books is consistent with the whole, making the Bible really one story by one ultimate author — God himself.

The Bible is divided into two testaments. The Old Testament contains thirty-nine books, mostly written in Ancient Hebrew with some portions in Aramaic. It begins with creation in the book of Genesis and ends with the rebuilding of the Temple in 430 BC. Using various kinds of books — historical narrative, poetry, and prophecy — it tells the history of God's relationship with his chosen people, the nation of Israel.

---

3 "What Do Americans Really Think About the Bible?" Barna Group, 2013.

The New Testament contains twenty-seven books originally written in Ancient Greek, in the form of historical narratives and letters (also called epistles). The letters are further divided into Pauline Letters (i.e. letters written by Paul) and General Letters, written by anyone else. The storyline of the New Testament starts 400 years after the last writings of the Old Testament (known as the 400 years of silence) with the birth of Jesus. It tells of the life of Jesus and the history of God's chosen people, the Church, ending with the future restoration of all creation.

It's critical for us to remember that the Bible we hold in our hands is not merely a collection of ancient stories, poems, and letters written by people in a different time, a different language, and a dramatically different culture. It is God's inspired Word to us today. At Clear Creek Community Church, this is one of our Essential Beliefs:

> The Bible is God's Word. It was written by human authors, under the supernatural guidance and inspiration of the Holy Spirit. It is the supreme source of truth for Christian beliefs and living. Because the Bible is inspired by God, it is the truth without any mixture of error.

When you open the Bible, God opens his mouth. God speaks. You get to communicate with the all-powerful, invisible Creator of the universe and lover of your soul. In the Bible, we get to know what God is like, what he wants, and what he is doing in the world. Reading the Bible daily is a habit that impacts everything else. The purpose of the next seven weeks is simple: to inspire and equip you to read, study, and apply the Bible daily. God speaks through the Bible.

Questions for Reflection

How often do you read the Bible? What has formed and shaped your Bible-reading habit (or lack thereof)?

____

____

____

How much of your worldview is influenced by what God says in the Bible? In what ways is that evident to those around you?

____

____

____

What has deterred you in the past from regular Bible reading? How can your group's accountability motivate you?

____

____

____

Prayer

Praise God for the beauty of his word, aware that he didn't have to reveal himself to us at all. Repent of any past neglect of your time with him, and ask him to help you as you strive to establish a daily habit of time in his word.

SCRIPTURE MEMORY

All________is breathed out by God and profitable for teaching, for reproof, for correction, and for training in righteousness, that the man of God may be complete, ________for every good work. *–2 Timothy 3:16-17*

THE AUTHORITY OF THE BIBLE

Scripture Study

Luke 24:13-27

That very day two of them were going to a village named Emmaus, about seven miles from Jerusalem, [14] and they were talking with each other about all these things that had happened. [15] While they were talking and discussing together, Jesus himself drew near and went with them. [16] But their eyes were kept from recognizing him. [17] And he said to them, "What is this conversation that you are holding with each other as you walk?" And they stood still, looking sad. [18] Then one of them, named Cleopas, answered him, "Are you the only visitor to Jerusalem who does not know the things that have happened there in these days?" [19] And he said to them, "What things?" And they said to him, "Concerning Jesus of Nazareth, a man who was a prophet mighty in deed and word before God and all the people, [20] and how our chief priests and rulers delivered him up to be condemned to death, and crucified him. [21] But we had hoped that he was the one to redeem Israel. Yes, and besides all this, it is now the third day since these things happened. [22] Moreover, some women of our company amazed us. They were at the tomb early in the morning, [23] and when they did not find his body, they came back saying that they had even seen a vision of angels, who said that he was alive.²⁴ Some of those who were with us went to the tomb and found it just as the women had said, but him they did not see." ²⁵ And he said to them, "O foolish ones, and slow of heart to believe all that the prophets have spoken! ²⁶ Was it not necessary that the Christ should suffer these things and enter into his glory?" ²⁷ And beginning with Moses and all the Prophets, he interpreted to them in all the Scriptures the things concerning himself.

Observing the text

Based on verses 13-14, what is the context of this passage (what has just happened)? What verses tell us why these two disciples are so devastated?

____

____

____

Based on verses 17-24, why are the disciples taken back with Jesus' questions?

____

____

____

Interpreting the text

Why do you think Jesus kept them "from recognizing him"? How does the rest of the story give us hints as to his reasoning?

____

____

____

What does their description of Jesus tell you about their faith?

____

____

____

Teaching

If you want to read the Bible well, the single most important thing you must do is recognize and submit to its authority. You can read the Bible cover-to-cover a few times each year, know every verse by heart, and study the original languages, but a Christian who does not recognize and submit to the authority of the Bible is no different from the Pharisees whom Jesus denounced.

> _Woe to you, scribes and Pharisees, hypocrites! For you are like whitewashed tombs, which outwardly appear beautiful, but within are full of dead people's bones and all uncleanness. So you also outwardly appear righteous to others, but within you are full of hypocrisy and lawlessness._
>
> Matthew 23:27-28

The Pharisees were so well-versed in the Scriptures that they invented additional rules and regulations to follow because the 613 in the Old Testament weren't enough. They had the entire Old Testament memorized — yes, the entire Old Testament. Rigorous study changed their outward appearance and behavior, yet Jesus spoke these harsh words towards them because their devotion to the Law had little impact where it truly mattered. Their hearts were full of pride and an unwillingness to submit to the authority of the God revealed by the Scriptures they so meticulously studied.

Like the Pharisees, we struggle with authority in our own way. A 2015 Harvard survey on the Millennial generation's view of societal institutions in America showed that the media is the least trusted institution with 88 percent of millennials saying they only "sometimes" or "never" trust the press. Wall Street, Congress, and the President all got low marks for trustworthiness as well. But this isn't just the sentiment of millennials. Surveys across all generations show consistent findings: we simply don't trust authority.[1]

Frankly, it's easy to see why our culture is cynical about authority. We've seen or even been at the receiving end of abused authority by politicians, law enforcement, parents, bosses, and pastors. Although most individuals within these groups may wield their authority responsibly, we tend to only remember the headlines or personal experiences involving the irresponsible ones. As a result, even mentioning the word authority leaves a bad taste in our mouths. However, there can be tremendous negative consequences when we transfer this latent distrust of authority to our King and his word.

2 Timothy 3:16 says, "All Scripture is breathed out by God," which means God inspired the authors of the Bible to write the words he wanted there. From Genesis to Revelation, it is God's word for us. The King has communicated to the citizens of his kingdom, and Christians have always kept the Bible central to who they are and what they do.

For many (if not most) people, our struggle with the authority of the Bible is not about the trustworthiness of the Bible itself, but whether we really trust God and submit to him as our king. Who is going to be the king in your life? If we're honest, we want to be our own king. We like being in

---

1 Cillizza, Chris. "Millennials Don't Trust Anyone. That's a Big Deal." *The Washington Post,* WP Company, 30 Apr. 2015, www.washingtonpost.com/news/the-fix/wp/2015/04/30/millennials-dont-trust-anyone-what-else-is-new/.

control and not having to submit to someone else. We get to be the final authority, where our desires rule and our emotions determine truth. But this illusion of power will keep us from experiencing the kingdom we've been invited to join.

When we read and study the Bible, we don't approach it as a passive object to be examined where we cut it open and look around inside. With that method, the Bible tends to be changed by our examination of it. Rather, the Bible examines us. The truth of God's word cuts us open and looks around in our hearts, changing us from the inside out. The response of a follower of Jesus cannot be merely confessing that the Bible is true, it must also include a willingness to obey the truth of the Bible. Recognizing and submitting to the authority of the Bible means that when God speaks, we *Listen & Obey.* We are citizens of his kingdom, and if God is truly your King, you will submit to his voice. As Peter proclaimed, "Lord, to whom shall we go? You have the words of eternal life." (John 6:68)

Questions for Reflection

Do you agree or disagree with the statement, "If you want to read the Bible well, the single most important thing you must do is recognize and submit to its authority"? How does a recognition of the Bible's authority impact our response to it?

____

____

____

Why does it become problematic when someone claims to be a follower of Jesus but picks and chooses what he or she likes in the Bible? What passages or teachings in the Bible are you tempted to ignore?

____

____

____

How is recognizing the authority of the Bible ultimately an issue of who will be King in our lives? How have you seen this play out in your own experience?

____

____

____

Prayer

Pray for a submissive heart that willingly and joyfully recognizes the authority of God's word in all areas of your life. Ask him to examine, dissect, and expose your heart so that you might honor him with your desires and glorify him with your actions.

SCRIPTURE MEMORY

All Scripture is____________by God and profitable for teaching, for reproof, for correction, and for training in____________, that the man of God may be________, equipped for every good work. *–2 Timothy 3:16-17*

THE STORYLINE OF THE BIBLE

Scripture Study

Luke 24:13-27

That very day two of them were going to a village named Emmaus, about seven miles from Jerusalem, [14] and they were talking with each other about all these things that had happened. [15] While they were talking and discussing together, Jesus himself drew near and went with them. 16 But their eyes were kept from recognizing him. [17] And he said to them, "What is this conversation that you are holding with each other as you walk?" And they stood still, looking sad. [18] Then one of them, named Cleopas, answered him, "Are you the only visitor to Jerusalem who does not know the things that have happened there in these days?" [19] And he said to them, "What things?" And they said to him, "Concerning Jesus of Nazareth, a man who was a prophet mighty in deed and word before God and all the people, [20] and how our chief priests and rulers delivered him up to be condemned to death, and crucified him. [21] But we had hoped that he was the one to redeem Israel. Yes, and besides all this, it is now the third day since these things happened. [22] Moreover, some women of our company amazed us. They were at the tomb early in the morning, [23] and when they did not find his body, they came back saying that they had even seen a vision of angels, who said that he was alive. [24] *Some of those who were with us went to the tomb and found it just as the women had said, but him they did not see." [25] And he said to them, "O foolish ones, and slow of heart to believe all that the prophets have spoken! [26] Was it not necessary that the Christ should suffer these things and enter into his glory?" [27] And beginning with Moses and all the Prophets, he interpreted to them in all the Scriptures the things concerning himself.*

Observing the Text

What parts of Scripture does Jesus refer these disciples to?

____

____

____

According to Jesus, what did the prophets say would happen to the Christ?

____

____

____

Interpreting the Text

Read Isaiah 53. How does Jesus fulfill this prophecy?

____

____

____

What claims does Jesus make about himself?

____

____

____

Teaching

The Bible is a complex book filled with stories, characters, and statements that at times can feel disconnected or irrelevant. What do we do with it all? Is it merely a useful book of moral teachings and rules to follow? Are the stories included just to give us examples of how to please God and go to heaven?

When it comes to understanding the overarching story of the Bible, one of the most amazing and instructive passages of Scripture is Luke 24:13-27. An encounter between the resurrected Christ and two of his confused, discouraged followers results in Jesus giving these guys an incredibly illuminating Bible study. His response to them makes it clear that Jesus viewed the entire Bible as being about him.

> *And beginning with Moses and all the Prophets, he interpreted to them in all the Scriptures the things concerning himself.*
>
> Luke 24:27

We might assume rightly the Gospel of Luke is all about Jesus — maybe even the whole New Testament. But is the Old Testament really all about Jesus too? Jesus has no doubts. He walks through "Moses and all the Prophets," delineating how it all ultimately points toward him.

The whole Bible, cover to cover, is a story that revolves around and culminates in one person: Jesus.

We will inevitably read the Bible through a certain lens. If you think the Bible is primarily about you becoming a moral person, then you're going to read the Bible looking for things to do. With this lens in place, you will see the stories in the Bible as lessons in how to be a good person and might even conclude that salvation is a result of being good enough for Jesus. A faulty lens can skew your view of the gospel itself.

With this lens in place, you'll also likely read yourself into every story, attempting to identify with the main characters. You might read about David defeating Goliath in 1 Samuel 17 and hastily determine that if we have enough faith like David, we can defeat our "giants" in life. Then you close the Bible and head out, hoping for enough faith to slay those giants: to beat cancer, to get a new job, or whatever else you've deemed your biggest obstacle.

If the story of David and Goliath becomes normalized for the everyday Christian experience and is merely about us defeating our giants, the pressure is on us to perform now. We better make it work. If your giants don't fall, you must not have enough faith in God, and you may even end up blaming God for not coming through like he did for David. Conversely, if your giants do fall, you emerge as the hero of the story.

When the Bible is viewed through a faulty lens, we find ourselves having to moralize, normalize, or spiritualize every story so that it fits us in a one-to-one ratio. This kind of reading risks misunderstanding what God is really trying to tell us.

What if we were to read the Bible like Jesus read the Bible? When Jesus flipped through the Bible, he didn't see a collection of moralistic fables primarily all about us. His lens displayed a story about God seeking to redeem and restore all things through the person and work of Jesus.

Let's take a second look at David and Goliath, and this time let's look through the lens of Jesus. Our first question: What's the context? When we read the surrounding text, we recognize that God's people are facing foes they cannot defeat. Goliath is their enemies' champion, is calling out for an equal representative from God's people to battle in a winner-takes-all death match. 1 Samuel 17:11 says, "When Saul and all Israel heard these words of the Philistine, they were dismayed and greatly afraid." No one, not even the king, can defeat this enemy with earthly might.

How does God respond to Goliath's challenge? He chooses a boy as Israel's champion. King Saul tries to give him his own armor, but David refuses it. Surely this small, untrained boy will be no match for the great warrior, Goliath. That's the point: man cannot beat this enemy, but God can. David is the only one in the story who understands this truth.

> *You come to me with a sword and with a spear and with a javelin, but I come to you in the name of the Lord of hosts, the God of the armies of Israel, whom you have defied. This day the Lord will deliver you into my hand, and I will strike you down and cut off your head...that all this assembly may know that the Lord saves not with sword and spear. For the battle is the Lord's, and he will give you into our hand.*
>
> 1 Samuel 17:45-47

David isn't the hero of the story — only God deserves that title. God raises up for his people a champion who will defeat an enemy they cannot and transfer the benefits of that victory to his people, though they didn't do anything to accomplish it. This isn't a story about us and our need for faith; it's the story of how God comes through in spite of our faithlessness. He saves because he is strong to save.

Viewed through the lens of Jesus, the narrative of David and Goliath provides a glimpse of a greater champion — the one whom God will provide to defeat an enemy his people cannot and transfer the benefits of that victory by faith to his people, though they didn't do any good works to earn it. Is it any wonder Jesus is called the Son of David? He has achieved a victory for his people which they never could. The story of David and Goliath is ultimately a story about Jesus.

Reading the Bible through Jesus' lens leads us to worship him with joy and gratitude. It both removes the anxiety and pressure to perform and simultaneously moves us to greater faith in God.

The original Star Wars trilogy revealed that Darth Vader was really Anakin Skywalker, Luke Skywalker's father, who turned to the Dark Side only to be saved from it at the end. When the prequel trilogy was released sixteen years later, knowing the story's ending changed the way we watched. Rather than being ruined by a lack of suspense, the foreshadowing, symbolism, and storyline were given deeper meaning, enhancing our understanding and appreciation.

Once we know that the Bible's story ends with the resurrection of Jesus, we can make better sense of what was happening with the people and events that preceded him. We can see these stories the way they ultimately are meant to be understood, through the lens of Jesus.

We must learn to read the Bible in reverse. Because we stand on the other side of the cross and know the end of the story, we should read the entire Bible in light of its expectation of Jesus: the true King, the true Priest, the true Lamb of God, the champion who will undo the fall in Genesis and bring us into the perfect kingdom found in Revelation. Reading the Bible in light of Jesus will enhance our understanding and appreciation for the story, while growing our love for its true hero.

Practically speaking, how can we remove the lens of self and look through the lens of Jesus? When reading your Bible, try asking yourself the following questions:

1. How does this story move us along in the story to Jesus?

2. How does this verse point us to the greater person and work of Jesus?

3. Where do we see our sin and the Lord's power to save?

4. How does this passage make us hungry for Jesus?

Asking these kinds of questions will begin to train you to see the Bible through the lens that Jesus used on the road to Emmaus — a book pointing toward, centered on, and all about Him.

Questions for Reflection

What other Bible stories have you read with the aim of finding a moral lesson? How might those stories ultimately point to Jesus?

____

____

____

If the Bible is ultimately a story that culminates in the person and work of Jesus, how can we see glimpses of him even in the Old Testament stories?

____

____

____

With what lens have you generally read the Bible and seen Jesus' place in it? What challenged your way of thinking in this study?

____

____

____

Prayer

Praise the Father who sent a champion to save us, the Son who achieved the victory on our behalf, and the Spirit who gives us the lens to see Jesus in the story. Pray that God would display his character and work on every page, leading us to obedience, worship, and joy.

WEEKLY EXERCISE

UNDERSTANDING THE STORYLINE

When we read an encyclopedia (remember those?), we ignore the article before and after the one we looked up, because they have nothing to do with the topic you're reading about. Encyclopedias are organized alphabetically and not with a story in mind. They are meant to be read without consideration for the context of the article. You can't read the Bible that way. The Bible is not a collection of random alphabetical topics but rather a story of God's restoration of the world, organized by the history of redemption. We can't understand an episode without understanding the whole story. To know the Bible, we must know the Grand Story it tells: the story of God and his plan of redemption in history.

Like any narrative, the Bible has a plot, a sequence of events that make up the story. Knowing the plot of the Bible is the first step in seeing how all of scripture is ultimately about Jesus. The aim of this exercise is to help you remember the plot of the Bible.

Place the following Biblical events in order chronologically:

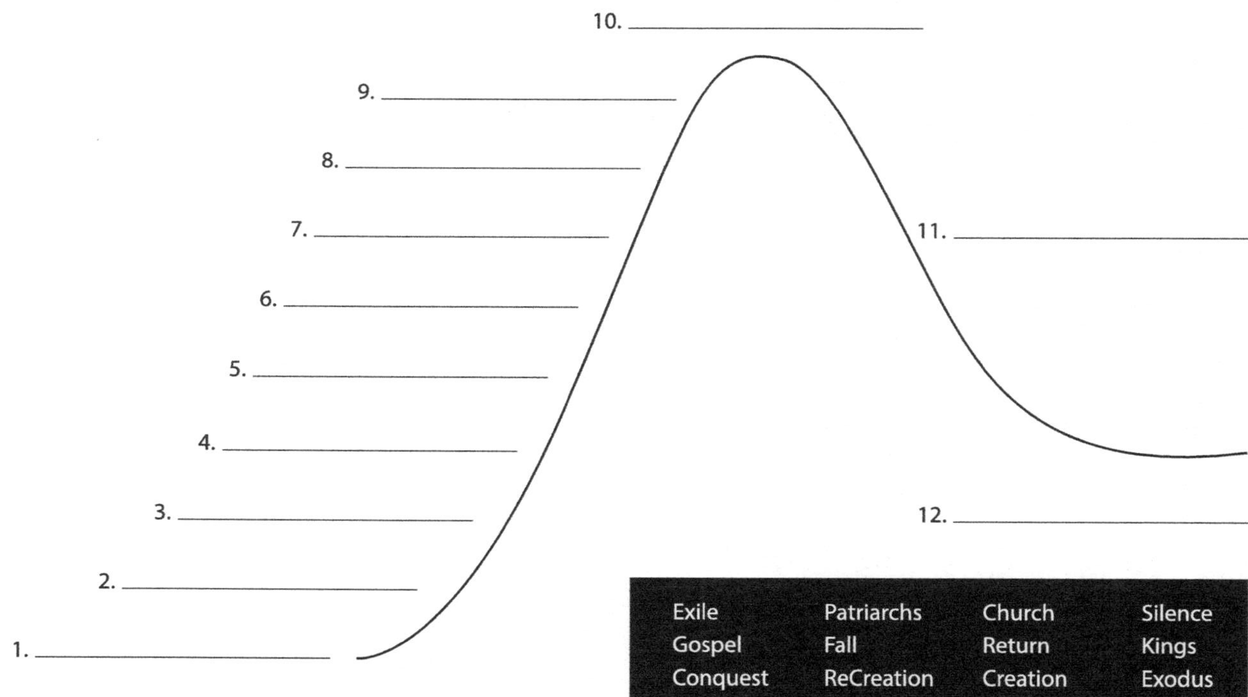

Creation, Fall, Patriarchs, Exodus, Conquest, Kings, Exile, Return, Silence, Gospel, Church, Recreation

Get Ready for Group

Write your memorized Scripture.

____

____

____

____

What observations and interpretations of Scripture were most meaningful to you?

____

____

____

____

____

Summarize your key takeaway(s) for this week.

____

____

____

____

What will you tell the group about the results of your exercise this week?

____

____

____

____

____

How has this week helped you better understand and apply the Spiritual Growth Grid?

____

____

____

____

____

REPENT & BELIEVE

WHO GOD IS	WHAT GOD DID	WHO WE ARE	WHAT WE DO
KING	CALLED	CITIZENS	LISTEN & OBEY
FATHER	ADOPTED	FAMILY	LOVE & SERVE
SAVIOR	SENT	MISSIONARIES	GO & MULTIPLY

04

READING THE BIBLE

SCRIPTURE MEMORY

All Scripture is breathed out by God and profitable for teaching, for reproof, for correction, and for training in righteousness, that the man of God may be complete, equipped for every good work. *–2 Timothy 3:16-17*

THE PROCESS OF DEVOTIONAL READING

Scripture Study

Psalm 1:1-6

Blessed is the man
    who walks not in the counsel of the wicked,
nor stands in the way of sinners,
    nor sits in the seat of scoffers;
2 but his delight is in the law of the LORD,
    and on his law he meditates day and night.
3 He is like a tree
    planted by streams of water
that yields its fruit in its season,
    and its leaf does not wither.
In all that he does, he prospers.
4 The wicked are not so,
    but are like chaff that the wind drives away.
5 Therefore the wicked will not stand in the judgment,
    nor sinners in the congregation of the righteous;
6 for the LORD knows the way of the righteous,

but the way of the wicked will perish.

Observing the Text

According to verses 1-2, what does the life of the "blessed" man look like? What does he avoid? What does he love?

____

____

____

What plants are used as metaphors for the "blessed" (verse 3) and the "wicked" (verse 4)? What characteristics of those plants does the writer highlight?

____

____

____

According to verse 2, why does a blessed man meditate on the law of the LORD day and night?

____

____

____

Interpreting the Text

What does the Psalmist say is a contributing characteristic of someone who prospers?

____

____

____

How is reading and meditating on God's word related to prospering? Do you think this is a promise from God? Why or why not?

____

____

____

What do you think about when you hear the word "delight"? What are the delights in your life?

____

____

____

Teaching

This week we will learn how to read the Bible devotionally. People may call this a "quiet time" or "daily devotional." Whatever you call it, it is time intentionally set aside to hear from God. Reading the Bible devotionally consists of reading and reflecting on a passage of Scripture to help focus your thoughts and guide your prayer.

Like any spiritual discipline, there is the danger of learning the *how* while neglecting the *why*. It is possible to create a plan and develop a daily discipline for reading the Bible and yet see little to no spiritual growth. As we pointed out before, the Pharisees of Jesus' day were guilty of going through the motions, doing religious activities (including daily Bible reading) while remaining hard-hearted toward God himself. Unless we see the delightful worth of his word, we will be prone to go through the motions, resulting in frustration when our spiritual growth is stunted.

Psalm 1 describes a person who is guided by God rather than following the wisdom of the age. He is called a "blessed" man. Verse 2 declares that *"his delight is in the law of the LORD, and on his law he meditates day and night."* The blessed person spends regular time reading and meditating on the word of God, because it is the delight of their heart. It's important to note that meditating on Scripture is more than just reading words on a page to increase our knowledge. Meditating on Scripture is a prayerful exercise of reading and reflecting on what God has spoken through his word.

We see this modeled by Jesus himself. Mark 1:35 describes him *"rising very early in the morning, while it was still dark, he departed and went out to a desolate place, and there he prayed."* Jesus made a regular habit of removing himself from the busyness of life and ministry to spend time praying and hearing from God. It only makes sense that we would model our lives after the example of Jesus, maintaining a regular rhythm of spending time with God.

But the truth is, reading the Bible can seem like an overwhelming endeavor at first. You may wonder where to start, how to understand it correctly, or what it means to apply it in your life. There are three questions that are helpful to ask as you read any passage of Scripture devotionally. Note that these questions will reappear next week when we discuss studying the Bible, because each is foundational to understanding and applying the word of God to your life.

1. What does it SAY?

The first question helps you to identify what stands out as you read. We call this *observation*. Adequately answering this question is essential for being able to dig deeper into the text with the next two questions. Use a journal or write directly in your Bible. You may need to read the passage a few times, underline repeated words or important points, and write down any questions you have.

2. What does it MEAN?

After asking what the passage says, you will begin to investigate its meaning. Now you are getting to interpretation. This question takes you beyond a literal, surface-level understanding of a text to now making sense of it. This requires you to think by drawing conclusions, making connections, and ultimately identifying the author's message. It may be helpful to look up some cross references or read the notes in a study Bible.

3. Why does it MATTER?

As you read and reflect on the Bible, God desires that you increase not only in knowledge, but also in likeness to Christ. This question is an opportunity to consider how you might pursue greater faithfulness to God in light of the text you just read. This may mean choosing a practice that will root truth more deeply in your heart or identifying an area where you need to grow in obedience. This is application. What will you do with what you have read?

The ultimate purpose of devotional Bible-reading is to deepen our relationship with God, rather than completing a duty. We will not garner extra divine favor for the day because we prayed and read the Bible that morning. We cannot earn our salvation by knowing the Bible better than others. That is putting *activity* before *identity*. In Christ, your identity is already established: you are a citizen of God's kingdom, not compelled by force to serve, but delighting in following him. As we begin to see him more clearly, we will more deeply desire to emulate his ways. One important way we do that is by setting aside daily time to prayerfully read and reflect on the Bible. You might find it helpful to have a journal alongside your Bible and examine each passage prayerfully. Consider what God is saying, what his words mean, and why it matters, trusting that he will illuminate his word for those who seek him there.

Questions for Reflection

What motivations have you had for reading the Bible in the past? Why do motives matter, and how do they indicate what we believe about our identity in Christ?

____

____

____

Why is it important to have a regular rhythm for reading and reflecting on God's word? What would it take for you to make that happen?

____

____

____

Which of the three questions is most challenging for you — observing, interpreting, or applying? Why is each step important to the process?

____

____

____

Prayer

Thank God that he desires a relationship with each of us, making a way through the cross and revealing himself to us in the Bible. Pray that he would make his great worth evident so that you might delight in the word.

SCRIPTURE MEMORY

All Scripture is breathed out by God and______________teaching, for re-proof, for correction, and for________ ______________, that the man of God may be complete, equipped for ______________. –*2 Timothy 3:16-17*

THE PRACTICE OF DEVOTIONAL READING

Scripture Study

Romans 6:1-14

What shall we say then? Are we to continue in sin that grace may abound? [2] By no means! How can we who died to sin still live in it? [3] Do you not know that all of us who have been baptized into Christ Jesus were baptized into his death? [4] We were buried therefore with him by baptism into death, in order that, just as Christ was raised from the dead by the glory of the Father, we too might walk in newness of life.

[5] For if we have been united with him in a death like his, we shall certainly be united with him in a resurrection like his. [6] We know that our old self was crucified with him in order that the body of sin might be brought to noth- ing, so that we would no longer be enslaved to sin. [7] For one who has died has been set free from sin. [8] Now if we have died with Christ, we believe that we will also live with him. [9] We know that Christ, being raised from the dead, will never die again; death no longer has dominion over him. [10] For the death he died he died to sin, once for all, but the life he lives he lives to God. [11] So you also must consider yourselves dead to sin and alive to God

in Christ Jesus.

[12] Let not sin therefore reign in your mortal body, to make you obey its passions. [13] Do not present your members to sin as instruments for unrighteousness, but present yourselves to God as those who have been brought from death to life, and your members to God as instruments for righteousness. [14] For sin will have no dominion over you, since you are not under law but under grace.

For the next two days, you will practice reading the Bible devotionally. Instead of reading and reflecting on a teaching section, you will study the provided passage using the SAY-MEAN-MATTER questions provided for guidance.

Observing the text — SAY

In the verses above, circle all references to death, and underline all references to life.

The words "with him" appear five times in this passage – fill in the blanks below.

- V. 4 - We were______________**with him**

- V. 5 - We have been______________**with him** in a______________like his.

- V. 5 - We shall certainly be________**with him** in a______________like his.

- V. 6 - Our old self was______________**with him**.

- V. 8 - We will also______________**with him**.

List out the *commands* you see in this passage.

____

____

____

There is a clear shift from statements about our spiritual standing before God to multiple commands. In what verse do you see this shift take place?

____

What are some words that would be helpful to define?

____

____

____

What other observations can you make about this text?

____

____

____

Interpreting the text — MEAN

How does Paul use the death and resurrection of Jesus as a parallel for our spiritual state?

____

____

____

How are the commands in verses 12-13 related to the previous statements in verses 1-11?

____

____

____

Write out Paul's argument in your own words.

____

____

____

Applying the text – MATTER

As you studied this passage what sin(s) in your life came to the front of your mind?

____

____

____

When you are tempted to engage in sin, what truth from this passage can you remind yourself of?

____

____

____

Prayer

Praise our crucified King who died that you might know him and be with him forever. Pray that he would open your eyes to see his message in the Scripture.

SCRIPTURE MEMORY

All Scripture is ________________

____and profitable for ______, for

______, for ________, and for _____

___ in righteousness, that the man of

God may be complete, equipped for

every good work. *–2 Timothy 3:16-17*

THE FURTHER PRACTICE OF DEVOTIONAL READING

Scripture Study

Romans 6:15-23

[15] What then? Are we to sin because we are not under law but under grace? By no means! [16] Do you not know that if you present yourselves to anyone as obedient slaves,[a] you are slaves of the one whom you obey, either of sin, which leads to death, or of obedience, which leads to righteousness? [17] But thanks be to God, that you who were once slaves of sin have become obedient from the heart to the standard of teaching to which you were committed, [18] and, having been set free from sin, have become slaves of righteousness. [19] I am speaking in human terms, because of your natural limitations. For just as you once presented your members as slaves to impurity and to lawlessness leading to more lawlessness, so now present your members as slaves to righteousness leading to sanctification.

[20] For when you were slaves of sin, you were free in regard to righteousness. [21] But what fruit were you getting at that time from the things of which you are now ashamed? For the end of those things is death. [22] But now that you have been set free from sin and have become slaves of God,

the fruit you get leads to sanctification and its end, eternal life. [23] For the wages of sin is death, but the free gift of God is eternal life in Christ Jesus our Lord.

Observing the Text - SAY

____

____

____

____

____

____

____

Interpreting the Text - MEAN

____

____

____

____

____

____

Applying the Text - MATTER

____

____

____

____

____

____

Prayer

Thank God that you are no longer enslaved to sin but have been given the gift of life forever with him. Ask him to continue to sanctify you through the reading of his word as you seek to understand and apply it daily.

WEEKLY EXERCISE

SCRIPTURE MEMORY

You have been asked to memorize Scripture throughout this study. Each week, as you meet with your group, you are asked to review and recite the passage for the week and some from the previous weeks. Why is memorizing Scripture worth your time and mental energy?

> Chuck Swindoll unequivocally affirmed the practice of memorization:

> I know of no other single practice in the Christian life more rewarding, practically speaking, than memorizing Scripture. …No other single exercise pays greater spiritual dividends! Your prayer life will be strengthened. Your witnessing will be sharper and much more effective. Your attitudes and outlook will begin to change. Your mind will become alert and observant. Your confidence and assurance will be enhanced. Your faith will be solidified.[1]

Memorizing Scripture helps fill the mind and heart of a citizen of God's kingdom with God's word. The myriad benefits of Scripture memory are difficult to overstate: it moves your heart to worship, helps you to discern God's will, encourages you in times of hardship, grounds you in the gospel as you fight sin, gives you words of counsel and encouragement for others, and guides your conversations as you engage unbelievers.

We live in an era when memorization is not necessary. Our knowledge is stored on gadgets, and a quick recall is only a few swipes away. Though you may find memorization laborious, it will pay off when you see God move in you. You will hear God's voice in your head as the Spirit brings to mind a passage you have memorized, giving you the right word at the perfect moment.

---

1 Chuck Swindoll, *Growing Strong in the Seasons of Life* (Grand Rapids: Zondervan, 1994), 61.

Write out each of your Scripture memory verses below:

Get Ready for Group

Write your memorized Scripture.

____

____

____

____

What observations and interpretations of Scripture were most meaningful to you?

____

____

____

____

____

Summarize your key takeaway(s) for this week.

____

____

____

____

What will you tell the group about the results of your exercise this week?

____

____

____

____

How has this week helped you better understand and apply the Spiritual Growth Grid?

____

____

____

____

____

REPENT & BELIEVE			
WHO GOD IS	WHAT GOD DID	WHO WE ARE	WHAT WE DO
KING	CALLED	CITIZENS	LISTEN & OBEY
FATHER	ADOPTED	FAMILY	LOVE & SERVE
SAVIOR	SENT	MISSIONARIES	GO & MULTIPLY

05

STUDYING THE BIBLE (PART 1)

SCRIPTURE MEMORY

My sheep hear my voice, and I know them, and they follow me. I give them eternal life, and they will never perish, and no one will snatch them out of my hand. *—John 10:27-28*

OBSERVATION: ASKING QUESTIONS

Scripture Study

1 Corinthians 13:1-13

If I speak in the tongues of men and of angels, but have not love, I am a noisy gong or a clanging cymbal. ² And if I have prophetic powers, and understand all mysteries and all knowledge, and if I have all faith, so as to remove mountains, but have not love, I am nothing. ³ If I give away all I have, and if I deliver up my body to be burned, but have not love, I gain nothing.

⁴ Love is patient and kind; love does not envy or boast; it is not arrogant⁵ or rude. It does not insist on its own way; it is not irritable or resentful; ⁶ it does not rejoice at wrongdoing, but rejoices with the truth. ⁷ Love bears all things, believes all things, hopes all things, endures all things.

⁸ Love never ends. As for prophecies, they will pass away; as for tongues, they will cease; as for knowledge, it will pass away. ⁹ For we know in part and we prophesy in part, ¹⁰ but when the perfect comes, the partial will pass away. ¹¹ When I was a child, I spoke like a child, I thought like a child,

I reasoned like a child. When I became a man, I gave up childish ways. [12] For now we see in a mirror dimly, but then face to face. Now I know in part; then I shall know fully, even as I have been fully known. [13] So now faith, hope, and love abide, these three; but the greatest of these is love.

Observing the Text

List all of the gifts and abilities that Paul describes in verses 1-3.

____

____

____

What attribute is said to be essential to their effectiveness?

____

____

____

What phrases does Paul use to describe utilizing these gifts while lacking that essential trait?

____

____

____

Interpreting the Text

Why is love essential to our implementation of spiritual gifts? How have you experienced the importance of love alongside ministry abilities (at church, with your small group, in your home)?

____

____

____

What does it look like when we "understand all mysteries and all knowledge" but lack love? How have you experienced this personally?

Teaching

Thus far we have discussed how to read the Bible devotionally, providing a framework to think through as you develop a regular rhythm of reading the Bible. You will soon see that the Bible is like the layers of the earth. As you dig deeper, there is more to see and learn about. Reading a passage might only whet your appetite to study it further, searching the infinite depths of God's revelation.

Studying the Bible is a spiritual endeavor. There is prayer at the beginning, prayer at the end, and prayer throughout. Trust the Holy Spirit to speak as you study, recognizing that he is the only source of the truth you desire to uncover.

However, studying the Bible also requires effort. We can't get away with passive, halfhearted attempts to learn. Don't be discouraged if you find some of this material difficult. Studying the Bible will require work, but like workout partners at the gym, your group is there to encourage and challenge you to grow.

Last week we introduced three questions to help you better read the Bible devotionally. Over the next five weeks we will learn to study the Bible using three steps based on those questions.[1]

---

1 The material found in chapters 5-9 have relied a great deal upon the works of Gordon D. Fee and Douglas Stuart, *How to Read the Bible for All Its Worth*, Fourth Edition (Grand Rapids, MI: Zondervan, 2014) and Howard Hendricks, *Living by the Book* (Chicago, IL: Moody Publishers, 2007).

1. **Observation** – What does it SAY?
2. **Interpretation** – What does it MEAN?
3. **Application** – Why does it MATTER?

Observation

> "I study my Bible as I gather apples. First, I shake the whole tree that the ripest might fall. Then I shake each limb, and when I have shaken each limb, I shake each branch and every twig. Then I look under every leaf. I search the Bible as a whole like shaking the whole tree. Then I shake every limb — study book after book. Then I shake every branch, giving attention to the chapters when they do not break the sense. Then I shake every twig, or a careful study of the paragraphs and sentences and words and their meanings." —Martin Luther

You've selected a passage, have your notebook or journal ready, and have prayed for God to speak. Now what? We begin with **Observation** (What does it say?). Think of yourself like a detective. At this stage in your study, you are merely observing things as they appear. You are looking for clues and connections, asking questions, and making notes of what needs further investigation. A good detective doesn't make any judgments or decisions at first; they simply look and take in everything their eyes can see.

At this point, do not reference any outside resources like a commentary or study Bible. Read the text, concentrate, and observe the text. Read it again. Observe some more. Now do it again! Keep on until you just can't get any more. Use a journal or write directly in your Bible. Underline main ideas, circle key phrases, write down connections you see, note repeated words or important points, and list out questions.

Begin your observation with what can be seen from a wide angle, like the setting and literary genre. Then progressively zoom in to the smaller and smaller details – paragraphs, sentences, phrases, and words. This will cause you to work your way through an established process that becomes automatic every time you look at Scripture.

The key to good observation is asking questions. Resist the urge to answer those questions at this point. You'll answer them in the next step. This is the time to question everything. Don't assume you already know the answer to anything. Imagine if you could submit a question to the author. What would you ask?

Think through the W's and the H.

WHO are the people involved? Who wrote this?

WHAT happened? What is the point? What is this about?

WHEN did this take place? When will future events occur?

WHERE did this happen? Where are they from?

WHY did this happen? Why did he say that?

HOW did this work? How did they get here?

Practice

Read Galatians 2:11-14 and write questions you have from the text using the W's and H (Again, no answers! Just questions.)

WHO?

____

____

____

WHAT?

____

____

____

WHEN?

____

____

____

WHERE?

____

____

____

WHY?

____

____

____

HOW?

____

____

____

Questions for Reflection

When it comes to studying the Bible, both relying on God and putting in effort are essential to success. Which of these is more challenging to you?

____

____

____

Why do you think it's important to not jump right into outside resources (like a commentary or study Bible)? What are the positive and negative impacts of using these tools?

____

____

Would you consider yourself an observant person? How difficult did you find it to practice this first step of studying the Bible?

____

____

____

Prayer

Ask God to give you a fresh reliance on him as you endeavor to study the Bible. Pray that he would give you wisdom, diligence, and faith to understand the words you read, and that those words would then transform your heart and life.

SCRIPTURE MEMORY

My sheep hear my______, and I know them, and they________me. I give them eternal life, and they will never ______, and no one will snatch them out of my hand. *—John 10:27-28*

OBSERVATION: FINDING PATTERNS

Scripture Study

1 Corinthians 13:1-13

If I speak in the tongues of men and of angels, but have not love, I am a noisy gong or a clanging cymbal. ² And if I have prophetic powers, and understand all mysteries and all knowledge, and if I have all faith, so as to remove mountains, but have not love, I am nothing. ³ If I give away all I have, and if I deliver up my body to be burned, but have not love, I gain nothing.

⁴ Love is patient and kind; love does not envy or boast; it is not arrogant⁵ or rude. It does not insist on its own way; it is not irritable or resentful; ⁶ it does not rejoice at wrongdoing, but rejoices with the truth. ⁷ Love bears all things, believes all things, hopes all things, endures all things.

⁸ Love never ends. As for prophecies, they will pass away; as for tongues, they will cease; as for knowledge, it will pass away. ⁹ For we know in part and we prophesy in part, ¹⁰ but when the perfect comes, the partial will pass away. ¹¹ When I was a child, I spoke like a child, I thought like a child,

I reasoned like a child. When I became a man, I gave up childish ways. [12] For now we see in a mirror dimly, but then face to face. Now I know in part; then I shall know fully, even as I have been fully known. [13] So now faith, hope, and love abide, these three; but the greatest of these is love.

Observing the Text

In verses 4-7, what does love look like? How is it displayed? Describe these attributes in your own words.

____

____

____

Which of these traits of love indicate an inward attitude?

____

____

____

Which traits of love indicate outward actions? (There may be some over-lap between the two groups.)

____

____

____

Interpreting the Text

Do these traits display love as a feeling or a choice? In what ways are both attitudes and actions essential to loving others well?

____

____

____

1 John 4:8 says that "God is love." In what ways have you experienced God's love in the form of the attributes in these verses?

____

____

____

Write out Paul's argument in your own words.

____

____

____

Teaching

As you carefully read your passage and make observations, you'll likely notice some patterns emerging from the text. Make note of these patterns; they are often intentional by the author. Here are five common patterns to look for in any particular Bible text:

Emphasized – What is given a lot of space in the text? What stands out?

Repeated – Are there any words, ideas or phrases that you see over and over?

Related – Do you see any connections between things you are observing? Did the author go from cause to effect?

Alike – Are there comparisons (ideas, words, etc.) in the text?

Unalike – Did the author contrast two things?

Practice

Read Romans 5:12-21 and write down any patterns you see.

EMPHASIZED

____

____

____

REPEATED

____

____

____

RELATED

____

____

____

ALIKE

____

____

____

UNALIKE

____

____

____

Questions for Reflection

Did you pray for God's help before you jumped into the practice passage? How will that habit impact the way that we study? What difference can it make when we seek the Spirit's help to understand his word?

____

____

____

What made this exercise challenging or simple for you? How has careful observation helped you to understand the Bible more effectively?

____

____

____

How can keeping God's perfect love in the forefront of our minds impact how we read the Bible? Did your reading of 1 Corinthians 13 affect how you experienced studying Romans 5?

____

____

____

Prayer

Thank God for any insight you gained as you studied today. He is the source of all true wisdom and knowledge. Pray that you would grow in godliness as you grow in understanding.

SCRIPTURE MEMORY

My sheep hear my voice, and I_____ them, and they follow me. I____ them________, and they will never perish, and no one will snatch them out of my hand. *—John 10:27-28*

OBSERVATION: GAINING PRACTICE

Scripture Study

1 Corinthians 13:1-13

If I speak in the tongues of men and of angels, but have not love, I am a noisy gong or a clanging cymbal. ² And if I have prophetic powers, and understand all mysteries and all knowledge, and if I have all faith, so as to remove mountains, but have not love, I am nothing. ³ If I give away all I have, and if I deliver up my body to be burned, but have not love, I gain nothing.

⁴ Love is patient and kind; love does not envy or boast; it is not arrogant⁵ or rude. It does not insist on its own way; it is not irritable or resentful; ⁶ it does not rejoice at wrongdoing, but rejoices with the truth. ⁷ Love bears all things, believes all things, hopes all things, endures all things.

⁸ Love never ends. As for prophecies, they will pass away; as for tongues, they will cease; as for knowledge, it will pass away. ⁹ For we know in part and we prophesy in part, ¹⁰ but when the perfect comes, the partial will pass away. ¹¹ When I was a child, I spoke like a child, I thought like a child,

I reasoned like a child. When I became a man, I gave up childish ways. [12] *For now we see in a mirror dimly, but then face to face. Now I know in part; then I shall know fully, even as I have been fully known.* [13] *So now faith, hope, and love abide, these three; but the greatest of these is love.*

Observing the Text

What gifts or abilities does Paul describe in verses 8-13 as temporary?

____

____

____

In contrast, what does Paul say will never end?

____

____

____

How do we "see" and "know" now? What will our seeing and knowing be like in eternity?

____

____

____

Interpreting the Text

Why do you think Paul describes the spiritual gifts as not lasting forever?

____

____

____

What do perfected "seeing" and "knowing" have to do with love, in contrast with faith and hope?

____

____

Teaching

Today you will start a study of Hebrews 4:14-16. Over the next few weeks we will continually come back to this passage and work through all the steps. We begin today with the first step: *observation*. First, pray for the Spirit's guidance. Then use the space provided to write out the "W's and H" questions and patterns you observe.

14 Since then we have a great high priest who has passed through the heavens, Jesus, the Son of God, let us hold fast our confession. 15 For we do not have a high priest who is unable to sympathize with our weaknesses, but one who in every respect has been tempted as we are, yet without sin. 16 Let us then with confidence draw near to the throne of grace, that we may receive mercy and find grace to help in time of need.

Questions for Reflection

In studying 1 Corinthians 13 this week, what connections did you see between that passage and the practice of studying your Bible? What motives should drive our study?

Did you feel prepared to observe the practice text today on your own? How are you approaching Scripture differently than you did before beginning this study?

How can your group help to hold you accountable to both diligent study and complete reliance on God? How can they encourage you to be led by love rather than simply seeking knowledge for the sake of pride?

Prayer

Take time to worship Jesus — our great high priest — who in his great love bears our burdens, believes in our future, hopes for our sanctification, and endured the cross for us. Pray that our love would become more like his as we daily behold him in the pages of his word.

WEEKLY EXERCISE

PERSONAL REFLECTIONS

Look back at your observations of Galatians 2:11-14 and Romans 5:12-21 of this week. Choose one of these passages and write some personal reflections. What insights did God give you in this passage? What relevance does this passage have for your life this week? How does what you learned further equip you to act in love this week, toward God or those around you?

Get Ready for Group

Write your memorized Scripture.

What observations and interpretations of Scripture were most meaningful to you?

Summarize your key takeaway(s) for this week.

What will you tell the group about the results of your exercise this week?

How has this week helped you better understand and apply the Spiritual Growth Grid?

____

____

____

____

____

06

Studying the Bible (Part 2)

SCRIPTURE MEMORY

My sheep hear my voice, and I know them, and they follow me. I give them eternal life, and they will never perish, and no one will snatch them out of my hand. *—John 10:27-28*

INTERPRETATION

Scripture Study

Matthew 4:1-11

Then Jesus was led up by the Spirit into the wilderness to be tempted by the devil. 2 And after fasting forty days and forty nights, he was hungry. 3 And the tempter came and said to him, "If you are the Son of God, command these stones to become loaves of bread." 4 But he answered, "It is written, "'Man shall not live by bread alone, but by every word that comes from the mouth of God.'"

5 Then the devil took him to the holy city and set him on the pinnacle of the temple 6 and said to him, "If you are the Son of God, throw yourself down, for it is written, "'He will command his angels concerning you,' and "'On their hands they will bear you up, lest you strike your foot against a stone.'"

7 Jesus said to him, "Again it is written, 'You shall not put the Lord your God to the test.'" 8 Again, the devil took him to a very high mountain and showed him all the kingdoms of the world and their glory. 9 And he said to him, "All these I will give you, if you will fall down and worship me."10 Then Jesus said to him, "Be gone, Satan! For it is written, "'You shall worship the Lord your God and him only shall you serve.'"

[11] *Then the devil left him, and behold, angels came and were ministering to him.*

Observing the Text

What similarities do you see between Jesus and what you might know about Israel in the Exodus?

____

____

____

How does Jesus respond to the devil's temptations?

____

____

____

Interpreting the Text

After crossing through the Red Sea, Israel wandered in the wilderness for forty years, often turning away from God when tempted in Exodus 14-40. Why is it significant that, after being baptized in the Jordan, Jesus is tempted in the wilderness for forty days and nights?

____

____

____

Why is it significant that Jesus rejects the devil's temptations by quoting Scripture?

____

____

____

Teaching

You've done your observations, and you're ready for the next step. We will spend the next three weeks learning about interpretation (what does it MEAN?).

It bears repeating at this point that studying the Bible should be a spiritual endeavor. While this step in the study process has the potential to feel somewhat technical and straightforward, we must always depend on the Holy Spirit to help us in understanding the Bible. Each of these steps must be covered in prayer so we remain sensitive to the Spirit's work in our hearts and minds.

With interpretation, we are trying to discover what the Bible means. Think of yourself like a scientist. After the observation step is complete, we then must discover the meaning behind it all. The aim of interpretation then is straightforward: find the author's original intended meaning.

For example, we want to know what Paul meant when he wrote Romans, what John was thinking when he penned his Gospel account, or what David's Psalms would have meant to the citizens of Israel.

This is contrary to the idea we sometimes hold that all interpretations are basically equal. Small groups often will gather around a passage as the leader asks, "What do you think that means?" And someone answers, "Well, to me it means..." More chime in, "To me, I think this means...because it just feels right to me." Everyone has their opinions, and everyone's opinion is regarded as equally "right for them."

That's not the purpose of studying the Bible. We seek to find not what the text means to us but what it meant to the Spirit-inspired human author.

They had a particular meaning for their readers, and as faithful Bible students we don't each get to determine our unique interpretations. That leaves us with three implications.

1. Generally speaking, each text has only one interpretation.

For example, Luke records Jesus' teaching of the Parable of the Lost Coin:

> *Or what woman, if she has ten silver coins and loses one coin, does not light a lamp and sweep the house and search carefully until she finds it? When she has found it, she calls together her friends and neighbors, saying, "Rejoice with me, for I have found the coin which I had lost!" In the same way, I tell you, there is joy in the presence of the angels of God over one sinner who repents.*

Luke 15:8-10

In telling this parable, Jesus had something very definitive he wanted to communicate to his original audience. Likewise, Luke recorded this parable to communicate that same point. If someone says, "This passage tells me that only men should handle the finances in the family because women have a hard time keeping track of money," they would be wrong. The parable is illustrating the depth of God's joy when his children repent and turn to him, just as someone would rejoice over finding something precious that had been lost.

As interpreters, we are seeking to discover the original meaning of the text. It's worth noting here that while there is generally only one way to interpret a text, we may derive many ways to apply a text.

2. A text cannot mean what it never meant.

If the original author had a specific meaning in mind at the time of their writing, then that will not change over time. What God intended to speak to his people when a text was written is what he meant to say. There is always the possibility, especially when it comes to prophecy and apocalyptic literature, that a text could find a secondary or later fulfillment. This will be discussed further when we cover those literary genres.

3. Simplicity is vital to interpretation.

If we're trying to find the original intent of the text, then what it says upfront is usually what it means. The simplest, most obvious answer is usually the right one. The original authors of the Bible were not writing puzzles containing hidden meanings that can only be solved using special knowledge. Gordon Fee notes:

> The aim of good interpretation is not uniqueness; one is not trying to discover what no one else has ever seen before... Unique interpretations are usually wrong...The aim of good interpretation is simple: to get to the plain meaning of the text. *The test of good interpretation is that it makes good sense of the text.*[1]

In the interpretation step, you will find it helpful to take advantage of some of the outside resources that are available to us. In the first step, we encouraged you to not use any outside resources but to simply make observations of the text on your own. We were asking questions of a text, but now we're trying to answer those questions. God has blessed us with a tremendous gift of access to an abundance of resources and tools that can help us understand his word. Biblestudytools.com has many free resources available.

Resources for interpretation:

- Different translations

---

1 Fee and Stuart, *How to Read the Bible for All Its Worth*, 17-18.

- Study Bibles
- Concordance
- Cross References
- Bible Commentaries
- Bible Handbooks & Encyclopedias
- Bible Atlas/Maps
- Bible Dictionaries

Questions for Reflection

Have you been in a group where everyone shared their personal interpretations for a passage as if they were all equally correct?

Why is it important to seek to discover the author's original intended meaning?

Write down any questions you have after reading this section.

Prayer

Take the time to repent of any arrogance in your previous study of the Bible — when you may have read the Bible with an insistence on your own opinion or context. Pray that God would help you to submit to his teaching as you study, for his honor and glory.

SCRIPTURE MEMORY

My sheep______________, and________ ______, and________________. I give them eternal life, and they will______ ______, and no one will snatch them out of my hand. *—John 10:27-28*

GRAMMATICAL CONTEXT

Scripture Study

Matthew 4:1-11

Then Jesus was led up by the Spirit into the wilderness to be tempted by the devil. ² And after fasting forty days and forty nights, he was hungry. ³ And the tempter came and said to him, "If you are the Son of God, command these stones to become loaves of bread." ⁴ But he answered, "It is written,

"'Man shall not live by bread alone, but by every word that comes from the mouth of God.'"

⁵ Then the devil took him to the holy city and set him on the pinnacle of the temple ⁶ and said to him, "If you are the Son of God, throw yourself down, for it is written, "'He will command his angels concerning you,' and "'On their hands they will bear you up, lest you strike your foot against a stone.'"

⁷ Jesus said to him, "Again it is written, 'You shall not put the Lord your God to the test.'" ⁸ Again, the devil took him to a very high mountain and showed him all the kingdoms of the world and their glory. ⁹ And he said to him, "All these I will give you, if you will fall down and worship me."¹⁰ Then

Jesus said to him, "Be gone, Satan! For it is written, "'You shall worship the Lord your God and him only shall you serve.'"

[11] Then the devil left him, and behold, angels came and were ministering to him.

Observing the Text

Why would the devil tempt Jesus with bread?

____

____

____

What does Jesus say is more "filling" than bread?

____

____

____

Interpreting the Text

Based on the devil's words, what does he believe about Jesus? What essential belief is the devil missing?

____

____

____

Why is bread alone not enough for people to truly live?

____

____

____

Teaching

When putting together a jigsaw puzzle, most people start by looking for the edges. With an easy-to-spot flat edge, we can quickly fit these pieces together to create the border for the puzzle, providing a framework for the rest. Once the border is complete, we still have a lot to do, but now we can start to work our way inward. We have a general sense of the overall picture.

When it comes to the process of putting the picture together of what a passage of Scripture means, knowing the surrounding framework is critical. It gives us the border from which we're able to start working inward. Too often, people jump to conclusions about a verse without considering the human author and original readers — their culture, language, historical background, or specific situation. These problems occur when we miss the greatest interpretative guideline in the study of Scripture: context.

Context literally means "that which goes with the text." Thomas Goodwin, an English Puritan theologian and preacher, famously said, "The right context of Scripture is half the interpretation." If we miss the context, most often we will misunderstand the text. There are three kinds of context that we will focus on:

> **Grammatical Context:** What is the meaning and placement of words?
>
> **Historical Context:** What is the time, culture and occasion?
>
> **Literary Context:** What genre of literature is this?

Grammatical Context

In determining the grammatical context, we want to know the meaning and placement of the words themselves. It is important to note no word or sentence stands alone. Every word is part of a phrase; every phrase is part of a sentence; every sentence is part of a paragraph; every paragraph is part of a chapter; every chapter is part of a book; and every book is part of the overall story of the Bible. It's crucial to understand not only the meaning of a word, but also how that word is being used in its sentence and how the human author uses that word elsewhere.

Word Study: Justify

Let's take a look at an example. James 2:24 says, *"You see that a person is justified by works and not by faith alone."* But, if we look at the writings of Paul we might notice an apparent contradiction. In Romans 3:28, Paul says *"For we hold that one is justified by faith apart from works of the law."* On the surface, it appears that Paul and James are making two opposing statements about what justifies a person: is it by works and not by faith alone, or is it by faith apart from works of the law?

There is a difference between what Paul and James say, but the difference isn't in their theology. The dissimilarity is how they use the word "justified." If you were to look up the word in a Bible dictionary, you would find that this Greek word can be used in two different ways.

Justify:

1. *To restore to a state of reconciliation with God those who stand under the judgment of his law.*
2. *To demonstrate or vindicate.*

What we see in Romans and James are examples of the two definitions. Using the first possible meaning, Paul states that the only thing that reconciles us to God is faith in Christ. James explains that true faith in Christ which reconciles us to God will always be demonstrated by works. Paul and James are not in contradiction, they are just addressing different issues and therefore emphasizing different points.

Grammar Review

Grammar may be something you were hoping you didn't have to remember past high school, but it is important when studying the Bible. The Bible is a literary work so it requires an understanding of how grammar works. The original languages of the Bible have been carefully translated so that, in most cases, the nuances of the grammar remain in the English translation. That should be great news, because it means you don't have to be a Greek or Hebrew scholar to study the grammar of the Bible. But you do need to know some English grammar concepts to help you maximize your study efforts. The following is a brief refresher course for those who might have forgotten!

Verbs

Verbs are words that describe an action. When you identify a verb in a sentence, ask yourself these questions to better understand what's happening in the passage.

What tense are they in (past vs. present vs. future)?

Is the action completed or continuous?

- Ephesians 2:8 – "For by grace you have been saved through faith…" *(completed)*
- 1 Corinthians 15:2 – "… and by which you are being saved…" *(continuous)*

Is it active or passive?

- Galatians 3:13 – "Christ redeemed us from the curse of the law…" *(active)*
- Romans 5:10 – "For if while we were enemies we were reconciled to God…" *(passive)*

Is it an imperative (command) or indicative (statement of fact)?

- Galatians 5:1 – "For freedom Christ has set us free *[indicative]*; stand firm therefore *[imperative]*, and do not submit again to a yoke of slavery. *[imperative]*"

What person is performing the verb?

	Singular	Plural
1st Person	I am	we are
2nd Person	you are	you are
3rd Person	he/she/it is	they are

Note: In English, 2nd person singular and plural appear the same (i.e. "you are"). However, this is not the case in Greek or Hebrew. In other words, they both have a word for "Y'all." You will need to use other tools and context to determine if the "you" in a passage is singular or plural in the original language.

Pronouns

A pronoun is a word that substitutes for a noun or noun phrase (i.e. you, he, she, his, her, who, which, these, those, etc.). There are different kinds of pronouns, but there is really only one question to answer: *to whom or what do they refer?* You must carefully read the passage and its surrounding context to help you. Let's look at an example from Colossians 2:11-12 to see why this is a big deal:

In him *[Christ, see v. 8]* also you *[the Colossian Christians]* were circumcised with a circumcision made without hands, by putting off the body of the flesh, by the circumcision of Christ, having been buried with him *[Christ]* in baptism, in which *[baptism]* you *[the Christians]* were also raised with him *[Christ]* through faith in the powerful working of God, who *[God]* raised him *[Christ]* from the dead.

Conjunctions

A conjunction is a word used to either connect clauses or sentences or to coordinate words in the same clause (i.e. and, but, for, yet, so that, since, therefore, in order to, etc.). Like pronouns, there are many different types but only one question to discern: *how are these paragraphs, sentences, or clauses related?* For example, when you see a paragraph begin with "therefore," you should automatically ask yourself, *what is that "therefore" there for?*

Here's an overwhelmingly long list of conjunctions: for, and, nor, but, or, yet, so, either/or, not only/but (also), neither/nor, both/and, whether/or, just as/so, after, although, as, as far as, as if, as long as, as soon as, as though, because, before, if, in order that, since, so, so that, than, though, unless, until, when, whenever, where, whereas, wherever, while, accordingly, additionally, again, as a result, finally, however, indeed, instead, just as, likewise, namely, nevertheless, now, otherwise, rather, similarly, that is, therefore, thus.

Congratulations, you made it through the grammar section! Developing (or rediscovering) a working knowledge of grammar will help you put the pieces of the context puzzle together as you study the Bible.

Questions for Reflection

How did the study on the word *justify* demonstrate for you the theological importance of studying grammatical context?

____

____

____

Review the two example passages for completed vs. continuous verbs and then look up Romans 10:9. What do these three usages of the verb "to save" teach you about salvation?

____

____

____

Write down any questions you have after reading this section.

____

____

____

Prayer

Thank God for giving us everything we need to understand his word: a translation into our own language, the intelligence and diligence that study requires, a community for insight and encouragement, and his Spirit to guide as we read. Pray that we would each faithfully seek to know him well.

SCRIPTURE MEMORY

My sheep hear my voice, and I know

them, and they follow me. ______

________________, and______________

______, and no one will snatch them

________________. *—John 10:27-28*

HISTORICAL CONTEXT

Scripture Study

Matthew 4:1-11

Then Jesus was led up by the Spirit into the wilderness to be tempted by the devil. 2 And after fasting forty days and forty nights, he was hungry. 3 And the tempter came and said to him, "If you are the Son of God, command these stones to become loaves of bread." 4 But he answered, "It is written,

"'Man shall not live by bread alone, but by every word that comes from the mouth of God.'"

5 Then the devil took him to the holy city and set him on the pinnacle of the temple 6 and said to him, "If you are the Son of God, throw yourself down, for it is written, "'He will command his angels concerning you,' and "'On their hands they will bear you up, lest you strike your foot against a stone.'"

7 Jesus said to him, "Again it is written, 'You shall not put the Lord your God to the test.'" 8 Again, the devil took him to a very high mountain and showed him all the kingdoms of the world and their glory. 9 And he said to him, "All these I will give you, if you will fall down and worship me."10 Then

Jesus said to him, "Be gone, Satan! For it is written, "'You shall worship the Lord your God and him only shall you serve.'"

[11] Then the devil left him, and behold, angels came and were ministering to him.

Observing the Text

What does the devil offer to Jesus in exchange for worshipping him?

____

____

____

What is different about the devil's third temptation?

____

____

____

Interpreting the Text

If Jesus is the King of kings and his glory surpasses all earthly kingdoms, why would he be tempted by the third temptation? In other words, what is the devil really offering Jesus?

____

____

____

Why doesn't the devil say, "If you are the Son of God..." in the third temptation?

____

____

____

Teaching

Around the corner from Trafalgar Square in London, near some of the embassies and high commission offices of countries all around the world, there once stood a restaurant called the Texas Embassy Cantina. Inside, the walls were decorated with kitschy Texas history and memorabilia. Though the restaurant no longer exists, people from all over the world would don cowboy hats, excitedly say "howdy" to the waiter, and order enchiladas, thinking they were getting the "real Texas experience." Any true Texans visiting London would take a photo outside but go eat somewhere else. A real Texan knows there's no place like home.

We know that history has certain boundaries within each time period – boundaries of language, dress, food, and culture. What is second nature for someone born in a particular place in a particular time is foreign to someone not from that historical context. As we approach the historical context of a passage of Scripture, we must ask ourselves: *what is the time, culture, and occasion?*

Our first responsibility is to acknowledge that we are foreigners to the historical context of the Bible. The way of life, geography, food, language, and stories that shaped their worldview were all second nature to those who lived at that time, but there's a gap of millennia between historical biblical culture and present-day society. As students of the Bible, we must bridge that gap and enter the world of the Bible so that we might understand how the text applies to us in our world.

Also, because the Bible was written over a period of 1,500 years, the historical context changes and evolves over time. Just like life for early Americans of the 1700s drastically differs from our experience today, the cultural background of Abraham was very different from those living in the time of Jesus. Likewise, the events of the Bible take place in locations spread from Egypt to Persia to Macedonia. The people of Galilee during Jesus' ministry had little in common with the citizens of the Roman colonies visited during Paul's missionary journeys. The *time, culture, and occasion* matters.

The Language Gap

As we think about the historical context of a passage, there are three gaps that we need to bridge from the Bible's world to ours. The first is the *language gap*. Every culture in history has spoken a distinct language. Languages evolve over time, developing unique idioms, expressions, and euphemisms. For those within that culture, the meanings behind specific words or phrases are widely understood without a second thought, even if they can't recount how that expression came to be.

There's not a day (or even a conversation) that goes by without hearing an expression particular to one's culture. *A little bird told me. Knock on wood. At each other's throats. Make a beeline. On the tip of my tongue. Stabbed in the back.* All of these are phrases that native English speakers in America commonly hear and use. But someone who speaks another language might struggle to understand the intended meaning.

In the same way, the cultures in the Bible each have their own idioms, expressions, and euphemisms. Most English translations will translate particularly confusing phrases, but there are plenty throughout the Bible that require some thought. Here are just a few examples to be on the lookout for:

"Adam knew Eve his wife" (Gen 4:1)............................. Sexual intercourse

"Abraham...was gathered to his people" (Gen 25:8)............................. Death

"Then your heart be lifted up" (Deut 8:14).................... To be become proud

"Tie up your garment" (2 Kin 4:29)... Get ready

"He stiffened his neck" (2 Chr 36:13) .... He became stubborn

The Culture Gap

The second gap we must bridge is the *culture gap*. Every culture has a set of customs, ideas, and philosophies that shape everyday life. A child setting up a lemonade stand on their curb has no idea how much capitalism, democracy, and the American Dream have impacted the concept of their new business venture. It might never occur to a child in a country with restricted access to the lemonade market to launch such a business. The customs, ideas, and philosophies of our culture are ingrained in us.

Everyday life in the Bible was filled with annual feasts, monthly observances, and daily rituals. All of this was as normal as the air they breathed. Consider this example from John's gospel:

> *On the last day of the feast, the great day, Jesus stood up and cried out, "If anyone thirsts, let him come to me and drink. Whoever believes in me, as the Scripture has said, 'Out of his heart will flow rivers of living water.'"*

John 7:37-38

If we've made our observations and noticed the emphasis on the specific day of the feast, with further research we might find that a water ritual was performed on the final day of the Feast of Tabernacles, asking God for rain during the following year. Jesus was using this ritual as a cultural touchpoint and offering himself as a better alternative.[1]

As we study the Bible, we also must remember that culture changes over time. In the past 1,500 years, we've gone from monks copying manuscripts by hand to the internet and the iPhone. We can assume that biblical culture changed in similarly unimaginable ways. Additionally, in any given time period of the Bible, we rarely see a homogeneous culture, meaning

---

1 Carson, D. A., et al. *New Bible Commentary: 21st Century Edition* (Downers Grove, IL: Inter-Varsity Press, 1998), 1041.

there is a mixture of rituals, customs, and philosophies.

For example, Paul often wrote letters to churches consisting of members from widely different cultural backgrounds. In one letter, Paul addresses the food laws of the Jews, while in another he addresses Greeks eating food offered to idols. Those are two very different audiences with very different ideas and customs pertaining to food. The challenge for students of the Bible is to understand and interpret how each cultural context influenced the underlying issues, and how the Bible's authors addressed these.

The History Gap

The final gap we must bridge to better understand the historical context of the Bible is the *history gap*. We must identify the specific historical events that affected or influenced the society. In every culture there is a narrative woven through historical events. Wars, conflicts, famines, and leadership transitions are just a few examples of events that shape how people think, talk, and behave, and we see many instances of those throughout Scripture.

For example, in John 4, Jesus engages in a lengthy dialogue with a Samaritan woman. A modern reader might gloss over her nationality as an interesting but immaterial detail, but in the original context this was a scandalous and outrageous scene for a "righteous" rabbi. John parenthetically helps us see that this is a big deal in verse 9, but an astute Bible student might ask of the text, "Why did Jews have no dealings with Samaritans?"

Further investigation using study Bible notes or commentaries would help us discover that much of the animosity between Jews and Samaritans in Jesus' day dated back almost 600 years. When the Jewish nation of Judah was being overthrown by the Babylonians, the Samaritans (who were of Jewish heritage) sided with the enemy. The Babylonians ultimately captured Judah, exiled most of the people, and moved in. The Samaritans intermarried with the Babylonians and mixed their religious practices. So to the Jews in Jesus' day, Samaritans were not only "half-breeds," but traitors, which is why "Jews have no dealings with Samaritans" (John 4:9).

As we seek to grow as students of God's word, we must understand the time, culture, and occasion of the text we read. In order to do that, we must immerse ourselves in the context so that we might bridge the gaps between our world and world of the Bible. Our goal is to know the world of the Bible as clearly as we know what it means to be a true Texan.

Questions for Reflection

How are you challenged by the recognition that the world of the Bible is different than the world of today?

____

____

____

How does Jesus' conversation with a Samaritan woman give you a picture of his grace towards you? How does it challenge you to treat others differently?

____

____

____

Write down any questions you have after reading this section.

____

____

____

Prayer

Praise the Father and Creator of all, our infinite and eternal King over every culture, language, era, and nation. Ask him to give you wisdom as you pursue a deeper knowledge of his work and character.

WEEKLY EXERCISE

THE CONTEXT OF HEBREWS 4:14-16

Let's continue studying Hebrews 4:14-16 by looking closer at the grammatical and historical context.

14 Since then we have a great high priest who has passed through the heavens, Jesus, the Son of God, let us hold fast our confession. 15 For we do not have a high priest who is unable to sympathize with our weaknesses, but one who in every respect has been tempted as we are, yet without sin. 16 Let us then with confidence draw near to the throne of grace, that we may receive mercy and find grace to help in time of need.

Grammatical Context

Begin by underlining the verbs and circling the conjunctions above. Next, draw a box around the two imperatives. (Hint: they are both first person plural imperatives so they start with "let us...")

Historical Context

Research the background of the priesthood in the Old Testament by looking up the following cross references and reading the "Christ as Priest" article in *Baker's Evangelical Dictionary of Theology* available by searching biblestudytools.com.

- Leviticus 16:21-22, 32-34
- Hebrews 7:26-28
- Hebrews 9:1-14, 24-26
- Hebrews 10:1-25

Write your reflections of the role of a High Priest and how it gives you a fuller understanding of Jesus.

Get Ready for Group

Write your memorized Scripture.

What observations and interpretations of Scripture were most meaningful to you?

Summarize your key takeaway(s) for this week.

What will you tell the group about the results of your exercise this week?

How has this week helped you better understand and apply the Spiritual
Growth Grid?

____

____

____

____

____

REPENT & BELIEVE

WHO GOD IS	WHAT GOD DID	WHO WE ARE	WHAT WE DO
KING	CALLED	CITIZENS	LISTEN & OBEY
FATHER	ADOPTED	FAMILY	LOVE & SERVE
SAVIOR	SENT	MISSIONARIES	GO & MULTIPLY

07

Studying the Bible (Part 3)

SCRIPTURE MEMORY

For the word of God is living and active, sharper than any two-edged sword, piercing to the division of soul and of spirit, of joints and of marrow, and discerning the thoughts and intentions of the heart. *—Hebrews 4:12*

LITERARY CONTEXT: LETTERS

Scripture Study

2 Peter 3:1-2, 15-18

This is now the second letter that I am writing to you, beloved. In both of them I am stirring up your sincere mind by way of reminder, ² that you should remember the predictions of the holy prophets and the commandment of the Lord and Savior through your apostles...

¹⁵ And count the patience of our Lord as salvation, just as our beloved brother Paul also wrote to you according to the wisdom given him, ¹⁶ as he does in all his letters when he speaks in them of these matters. There are some things in them that are hard to understand, which the ignorant and unstable twist to their own destruction, as they do the other Scriptures. ¹⁷ You therefore, beloved, knowing this beforehand, take care that you are not carried away with the error of lawless people and lose your own stability. ¹⁸ But grow in the grace and knowledge of our Lord and Savior Jesus Christ. To him be the glory both now and to the day of eternity. Amen.

Observing the Text

What is the author's purpose in writing and what does he say he is writing (verses 1-2)?

____

____

____

How has Paul shared his wisdom with the readers, according to the author?

____

____

____

How do the "ignorant and unstable" respond to Paul's teachings? How does this compare with their response to "the other Scriptures" (i.e. the Old Testament)?

____

____

____

Interpreting the Text

Who is the author? Who is his intended audience? (For a hint, look at 2 Peter 1:1 if needed)

____

____

____

What does the comparison between Paul's letters and the "other Scriptures" imply about the writing of Paul? What significance does this have concerning the validity of other New Testament books?

____

____

____

What is Peter encouraging his audience to do in this passage? How does he want them to think?

____

____

____

Teaching

When radio listeners tuned into CBS on October 30, 1938, a news bulletin interrupted the regular programming, reporting a series of odd explosions seen on Mars. Soon after, another news bulletin reported that an unusual spacecraft-like object had fallen from the sky in Grover's Mill, New Jersey. More reports came of alien spacecraft landings across the United States and the world. Heat ray-armed Martians were attacking earth. Unaware that the "news reports" were actually part of the fictional The Mercury Theatre on the Air radio program, listeners were terrified and mass hysteria ensued. The public's reaction to Orson Welles' on-air drama "The War of the Worlds" shows us what can happen when we confuse literary genres.

There's a world of difference between a news report and a fictional work, an email and a poem, a contract and a cookbook, or a tragedy and a text-book. These differences require us to read these works differently. There is a wide variety of literary genres, and each one has its own rules required to read it in the correct context. The Bible is no different. In order to better understand how literary context works, we will spend the next two weeks learning the interpretive keys for eight literary genres found in the Bible: Letter, Historical Narrative, Parable, Law, Prophetic, Apocalyptic, Poetic, and Wisdom (Proverbial).

Letter

Letters or epistles make up most of the New Testament books, including Romans, 1 & 2 Corinthians, Hebrews, and James among many others. Much like a formal letter today, the letters of the Bible use straightforward language, lead toward a specific point or points, and generally follow a set form.

The form of Ancient Letters:
I. Introduction
  a. Author ID
  b. Recipients ID
  c. Greeting
  d. Blessing/Prayer
II. Body - Addressing specific situation for intended community
III. Conclusion
  a. Travel plans
  b. Prayer
  c. Requests
  d. Greetings/Affection

Each individual letter may not contain every one of these elements in the introduction or conclusion, but you'll generally find them there (read Colossians 1:1-14 and Colossians 4 to see classic examples of an introduction and conclusion). Here are some strategies for reading and understanding the letters of the New Testament:

Read through the entire letter as you would a letter today. These letters were originally intended to be read aloud in the presence of the gathered church. By first reading through the entire letter in one sitting, you'll get a sense of the overall flow, tone, and main arguments of the letter.

Summarize the content of each paragraph. Modern translations provide paragraph breaks and section headings (which weren't in the original languages) to help readers better follow the flow of the letter. Take time to outline. What's the major point being made? How do the individual paragraphs contribute to the overall argument of the section or chapter? Try writing out a one-sentence summary of each paragraph.

Ask yourself: "What's the situation?" Each letter is written by a human author trying to apply theology in practical ways to a specific situation within a historical church setting. Letters in the Bible are not simply theological treatises. The writers of epistles were addressing a variety of questions or issues in churches such as persecution, death, sexual sin, money, slaves, family life, and government interaction. Awareness of their situation is crucial to correctly identifying what's being addressed.

Look for the main point(s) under discussion. A New Testament letter isn't a random collection of thoughts jotted down by the writer as they popped into his head. He has a purpose. Even the digressions, which may take a chapter or more before returning to the issue at hand, are always purposeful. Take the time to follow the arguments, examining how the author is working toward a main point or points.

Questions for Reflection

Outside of the Bible, what do you like to read? How does the genre of your reading material impact the way that you read it?

____

____

____

Which sections/genres of the Bible do you naturally gravitate toward? Which do you tend to avoid? What do you think is at the root of this habit?

____

____

____

Prayer

Thank God today for the myriad ways in which he chooses to communicate with his children in his perfect word. Pray that we would read with diligence, study with humility, and seek him without fear.

SCRIPTURE MEMORY

For the_______of God is living and

______, sharper than any two-edged

sword, piercing to the division of soul

and of spirit, of joints and of marrow,

and discerning the thoughts and in-

tentions of the______. *—Hebrews 4:12*

HISTORICAL NARRATIVES AND PARABLES

Scripture Study

Matthew 13:10-17, 34-35

Then the disciples came and said to him, "Why do you speak to them in parables?" [11] And he answered them, "To you it has been given to know the secrets of the kingdom of heaven, but to them it has not been given. [12] For to the one who has, more will be given, and he will have an abundance, but from the one who has not, even what he has will be taken away. [13] This is why I speak to them in parables, because seeing they do not see, and hearing they do not hear, nor do they understand.[14] Indeed, in their case the prophecy of Isaiah is fulfilled that says:

""You will indeed hear but never understand,

   and you will indeed see but never perceive."

[15] For this people's heart has grown dull,

   and with their ears they can barely hear,

   and their eyes they have closed,

lest they should see with their eyes

   and hear with their ears

and understand with their heart

and turn, and I would heal them.'

[16] But blessed are your eyes, for they see, and your ears, for they hear.[17] For truly, I say to you, many prophets and righteous people longed to see what you see, and did not see it, and to hear what you hear, and did not hear it.

[34] All these things Jesus said to the crowds in parables; indeed, he said nothing to them without a parable. [35] This was to fulfill what was spoken by the prophet:

"I will open my mouth in parables;

I will utter what has been hidden since the foundation of the world."

Observing the Text

Who is speaking in this passage? Who is his audience?

____

____

____

What question do the disciples ask Jesus?

____

____

____

How does Jesus describe the difference between his disciples and the crowds?

____

____

____

Interpreting the Text

In your own words, summarize Jesus' answer to his disciples' question.

____

____

How do parables both hide and reveal truth? In what way is this affected by who is listening?

____

____

____

Teaching

Today we will be discussing two different types of narratives. The word _narrative_ simply means a story or a series of connected events with characters, a setting, and a plot. Narratives can be classified as either fiction or nonfiction. The first type of narrative discussed today will be an example of nonfiction: _historical narratives_, telling a story of true events involving real people. We will then study _parables_, a unique type of fictional narrative.

Historical Narrative

Historical narratives are found in both the Old and New Testaments and include such examples diverse as Genesis, Exodus, 1 and 2 Samuel, the Gospels, and Acts. When you study a historical narrative, you must always step back and discern the overall plot. A story's plot includes the pattern or sequence of events that make up a story. The events in a story generally aim to accomplish some artistic or emotional effect.

If someone asked you what your favorite book or movie was about, your answer would probably follow the plot of the story. You would introduce the main characters and include important background information. You would tell them about the conflict that brought tension into the story. You would tell them about the rising action that ultimately resulted in the climax of the story. But you would assure them the story doesn't end there. There would still be important aspects of the story to be wrapped up, so you would tell them how the story ends.

Stories make greater sense to us when we know the plot, and the Bible is no different. Here are some key concepts to keep in mind when interpreting a historical narrative:

They usually do not teach a doctrine explicitly. Historical narratives usually illustrate a doctrine taught somewhere else. For example, in the narrative of King David committing adultery with Bathsheba in 2 Samuel 11, the words "adultery" and "murder" never appear. The reader is expected to understand that David's actions are morally reprehensible. The point of the story isn't to give a full explanation of the doctrine of marriage. However, it does illustrate the harmful consequences of adultery, murder, and deceit. The narrative is David's real life story, which includes his brokenness and need for redemption. Ultimately, it points to the great sinless king, Jesus.

They record what happened. Historical narratives do not necessarily record what should have happened. Therefore, not every narrative has an individual identifiable moral, especially the Old Testament historical narratives. They are not intended to teach moral lessons. The authors' purpose is to tell what God did in the history of Israel, not offer moral illustrations of right and wrong behaviors. They are historical narratives, not illustrative narratives.

There's a glaring problem with reading narratives as moral lessons with behaviors to imitate: the characters aren't always great examples of morality. Most narratives do not intend to hold up their human characters as models to be imitated (try reading the last five chapters of Judges and see if you can figure out whose example to follow!). The author's purpose is often to demonstrate how God accomplishes his purposes *in spite* of them, rather than *because* of them.

They are selective and incomplete. It's important to keep in mind that the historical narratives are literary retellings of actual events. Like any good storyteller, the biblical writers determine which details and events contribute to, or distract from the arc of their story. Much is left out[1] , but what does appear in the story is what God thought important for us to know. This ought to help us ask better questions in our observation step. *Why did the author include this seemingly insignificant detail? Are the excluded details meant to be implied, or are they irrelevant to the plot?*

They are not written to answer all of our theological questions. Historical narratives have specific, limited purposes and only deal with certain issues, leaving others to be dealt with elsewhere in other ways. In the creation account in Genesis 1-2, Moses wasn't composing a scientific thesis on genetics or biology, but rather, writing the beginning of the metanarrative of God and his redemption of the world through his people. You won't find answers to all your scientific and theological questions there. Instead, the main point of Genesis 1-2 is to leave the reader in awe of a God who created the universe and prepared a land for his people to live under his rule.

God is the ultimate hero of all biblical narratives. As we learned in week 3, the entire Bible — and therefore each story within it — is tied to the Great Story of God and his plan to redeem man. Human characters are flawed. Even when they get it right, God's gracious and sovereign hand is often highlighted, clearly reinforcing that all glory belongs to our God.

In the Gospels, many times the content was organized by topic working toward a central message. If you have read through the Gospels in the New Testament (i.e. Matthew, Mark, Luke and John), you may have noticed that the recorded chronology is different. These differences do not reflect an error in the Bible's accuracy but the authors' intentional ar-

---

1 John 21:25 reminds us, *"Now there are also many other things that Jesus did. Were every one of them to be written, I suppose that the world itself could not contain the books that would be written."*

rangements. When studying a Gospel, read through the entire book first, and if possible, in one sitting. Try to pick up on the author's central message. For a little help, use resources like the book's introduction found in a study Bible or commentary.

Parable

One of Jesus' favorite teaching styles was the parable. Parables are brief tales that illustrate moral principles using everyday matters familiar to the original listeners (e.g., farming, money, travel). Rather than complicated allegorical talks, they are simple, memorable, and designed to teach a clear lesson. While the majority of parables are told by Jesus, there are also parables found elsewhere in the Bible. 2 Samuel 12:1-6, Isaiah 5:1-6, and Ezekiel 17:3-10 are all examples of parables in the Old Testament. They are told as narratives but not historical.

Much like a joke, the parable is designed to drive home to its readers one point that stirs them. They are meant to provoke an immediate reaction. Thus, the parable will use images, people, or things that really strike at the original audience to emphasize the point.

The question you must always ask of a parable is "What's the main point?" Avoid pushing the metaphor to its breaking point by mining out too many lessons. At some point all metaphors will fall apart. The point of the Parable of the Lost Coin (Luke 15:8–10) is easy enough to understand. It's a picture of the "joy before the angels of God over one sinner who repents." If you base your banking practices on it, or use it to determine who in your family should be responsible for the budget, you've pushed the parable too far!

Questions for Reflection

What historical narratives in the Bible are difficult for you to understand or enjoy? How could the concepts taught today help you to read them differently?

____

____

____

How does it make you feel to consider that much has been left out of the Bible's historical narratives? Why is it important to remember this as we study?

____

____

____

Prayer

Praise our infinite, immortal God who is Lord over all the vast reaches of time and space. From the time before history existed to our eternal future with him, he has seen it and known it. He has never been and will never be surprised or overwhelmed. The great I AM, is also Immanuel, the God who is with us. Pray that his presence would shine through every page.

SCRIPTURE MEMORY

For the word of______is living and active,________than any two-edged sword,________to the division of soul and of spirit, of joints and of marrow, and discerning the thoughts and intentions of the heart. *—Hebrews 4:12*

LAW

Scripture Study

Deuteronomy 31:9-13

Then Moses wrote this law and gave it to the priests, the sons of Levi, who carried the ark of the covenant of the LORD, and to all the elders of Israel. [10] And Moses commanded them, "At the end of every seven years, at the set time in the year of release, at the Feast of Booths, [11] when all Israel comes to appear before the LORD your God at the place that he will choose, you shall read this law before all Israel in their hearing. [12] Assemble the people, men, women, and little ones, and the sojourner within your towns, that they may hear and learn to fear the LORD your God, and be careful to do all the words of this law, [13] and that their children, who have not known it, may hear and learn to fear the LORD your God, as long as you live in the land that you are going over the Jordan to possess."

Observing the Text

What does Moses do with God's Law? What does he command the priests to do with it?

____

____

____

Who needs to hear the Law?

____

____

____

Why do they need to hear the Law?

____

____

____

Interpreting the Text

Look at the context surrounding this passage to identify the setting. Where and when is this taking place? What impact does the setting have on what is happening?

____

____

____

When Moses says that the people of Israel will "learn to fear the LORD," does he mean that we should be afraid of God like some people fear snakes or heights? How would you explain the fear of the LORD in your own words?

____

____

____

Can you imagine a national holiday for reading the Bible? What does the establishment of this ceremony tell us about the importance God placed on studying his Law?

____

____

____

Teaching

The Old Testament contains more than 600 commandments which the Israelites were expected to obey. This Law of God is primarily contained in the material that starts with the Ten Commandments in Exodus 20, grows through Leviticus and Numbers, and concludes at the end of Deuteronomy.

For Christians today, reading the Law can be confusing. It may leave you wondering which laws God would have you obey and which laws are no longer binding on you. Some laws we seem to disregard, like the prohibition of eating pigs or shellfish (Deuteronomy 14:8-10) and wearing fabric of two types of material (Leviticus 19:19). Yet some laws we embrace, like the commands to love your neighbor as yourself (Leviticus 19:18), to not murder (Exodus 20:13), and to not commit adultery (Deuteronomy 5:18).

Why do we obey one law and not another? Which laws are valid today and which are not? You may have even gotten that question from a skeptical person, accusing you of picking and choosing which parts of the Bible to obey or ignore. Before you throw your bacon-wrapped shrimp in the trash and burn your polyester/cotton blend shirts, let's cover some concepts that will help us to more clearly interpret God's Law.

The Old Testament Law is a covenant between God and Israel. A binding contract between two parties, covenants were common agreements in the Ancient Near East used to define the relationship between kings of neighboring kingdoms. It has long been recognized by biblical scholars that the Pentateuch (the first five books of the Old Testament) resembles covenant documents of the second millennium BC. As part of the agreement, covenant documents included stipulations required to maintain the covenant. Obedience to the stated stipulations would result in blessings, while disobedience resulted in punishment. The more than 600 laws in the

Old Testament are the stipulations for God's covenant with Israel.

The Old Covenant is not our covenant. God's Old Testament covenant with his people Israel is not a covenant that followers of Jesus are part of today. In Christ, God made a New Covenant with the church (read Hebrews 8). Jesus tells us, "Do not think that I have come to abolish the Law or the Prophets; I have not come to abolish them but to fulfill them" (Matthew 5:17). By stating that he's the fulfillment of the Law, Jesus declares that every part of the Old Covenant ultimately points to him, and that he satisfies the requirements of the law on behalf of those who believe. Therefore they are no longer binding on us, except those aspects that are renewed in the New Covenant.

Some stipulations of the Old Covenant have clearly not been renewed in the New Covenant. There are three basic types of laws found in the Old Testament: civil, ceremonial, and moral. Two of these were specific to the theocratic nation-state of Israel and have clearly not been renewed in the New Covenant.

Civil Laws outlined for citizens of Israel which behaviors were subject to criminal prosecution and punishment. These laws also established how they were to care for vulnerable members of society. Jesus fulfilled the Law, but the New Covenant did not establish a theocratic nation-state for the church. So while the civil laws provide valuable wisdom for public governance (caring for the poor, etc.), they are not binding for the church today. For examples, read Exodus 22.

Ceremonial Laws provided instruction for carrying out the practice of worship in Israel. These laws established what behaviors made a person unclean, how that affected their participation in religious ceremonies, and the process for being restored to a state of cleanliness. These commands also instituted the authority structure and roles of the temple priesthood.

Jesus came to serve as the ultimate High Priest and fulfilled the ceremonial requirements of the Law for us. Now, we are counted as righteous before God. For examples, read some of the food laws found in Leviticus 11.

Part of the Old Covenant is renewed in the New Covenant.
Moral Laws commanded behavior that reflects God's character, defining what God considers good and evil, right and wrong. Some moral aspects of the Old Covenant law are actually restated or reapplied in the New Testament. Jesus either reaffirmed or intensified many of the moral laws both in the Sermon on the Mount (Matthew 5-7) and in his restating of the two great commandments (Matthew 22:40). Like the civil and ceremonial laws, Jesus is the fulfillment of the moral laws. Because of his work on the cross, Christians are not obligated to keep the moral law as a way to earn or maintain their salvation. However, because these laws reflect God's character and his views on morality – which do not change – followers of Jesus are called to obey the moral commands out of love for God. For examples, read the Ten Commandments in Exodus 20.

The Law is still the Word of God for us even though it's not the command of God to us. You might be tempted to skip reading the Law all together, thinking, "Jesus fulfilled it; so why read it?" The Bible, however, contains all sorts of commands that God wants us to know about, even if they are not directed toward us personally. Reading the Old Testament Law accomplishes at least two things in the heart of Christians today. First, it teaches you about the holiness of God. You can't help but be overwhelmed at the righteousness required by the Law. You will find yourself thinking, *Who could possibly keep all these?* Second, it enhances your worship of God as you reflect on the fact that he sent Jesus to "keep all these" because you and I couldn't. Reading the Law ought to increase your gratitude for the cross of Christ and overflow into worship.

Remember, Jesus fulfilled the Law. He is the new standard and interpreter for us! When you find yourself confused, look to Jesus. How did he view the Law? How did he interpret it for New Covenant believers? His perfect example will guide us into deeper understanding and a deeper faith.

Questions for Reflection

Which Old Testament laws have always seemed confusing to you? How does this lesson help you to come to a deeper understanding of those commands?

____

____

____

How does it feel to know that our salvation is not dependent on our ability to keep the Old Testament laws? Why is it important that we always reiterate that truth when we study the Law?

____

____

____

Have you ever been accused of picking and choosing which commands of God you obey? How might you answer this charge with more clarity than you could before today's lesson?

____

____

____

Prayer

Pray that your reading of God's commands would lead you into gratitude, praise, and love for our Savior who fulfilled all the Law. Thank him for the New Covenant, extending grace to those who were once his enemies.

WEEKLY EXERCISE

VARYING GENRES, VARYING APPROACHES

Look up the selected passages, identify the genre to which they belong, and put the principles in this week's lessons to work, interpreting them for believers today with a brief summary

2 Samuel 6:1-15

Literary Genre:

Summary Interpretation:

____

____

____

1 John 2:1-6

Literary Genre:

Summary Interpretation:

____

____

____

Numbers 19:11-13

Literary Genre:

Summary Interpretation:

____

____

____

Mark 12:1-12

Literary Genre:

Summary Interpretation:

____

____

____

Get Ready for Group

Write your memorized Scripture.

What observations and interpretations of Scripture were most meaningful to you?

Summarize your key takeaway(s) for this week.

What will you tell the group about the results of your exercise this week?

How has this week helped you better understand and apply the Spiritual Growth Grid?

____

____

____

____

____

REPENT & BELIEVE

WHO GOD IS	WHAT GOD DID	WHO WE ARE	WHAT WE DO
KING	CALLED	CITIZENS	LISTEN & OBEY
FATHER	ADOPTED	FAMILY	LOVE & SERVE
SAVIOR	SENT	MISSIONARIES	GO & MULTIPLY

08

Studying the Bible (Part 4)

SCRIPTURE MEMORY

For the word of God is living and active, sharper than any two-edged sword, piercing to the division of soul and of spirit, of joints and of marrow, and discerning the thoughts and intentions of the heart. *—Hebrews 4:12*

PROPHECY

Scripture Study

Jeremiah 1:4-9, 14-19

Now the word of the LORD came to me, saying,

[5] "Before I formed you in the womb I knew you,

and before you were born I consecrated you;

I appointed you a prophet to the nations."

[6] Then I said, "Ah, LORD God! Behold, I do not know how to speak, for I am

only a youth." [7] But the LORD said to me,

"Do not say, 'I am only a youth';

for to all to whom I send you, you shall go,

and whatever I command you, you shall speak.

[8] Do not be afraid of them,

for I am with you to deliver you,

declares the LORD."

[9] Then the LORD put out his hand and touched my mouth. And the LORD

said to me,

"Behold, I have put my words in your mouth.

[14] Then the LORD said to me, "Out of the north disaster shall be let loose

upon all the inhabitants of the land. [15] For behold, I am calling all the tribes of the kingdoms of the north, declares the LORD, and they shall come, and every one shall set his throne at the entrance of the gates of Jerusalem, against all its walls all around and against all the cities of Judah. ¹⁶And I will declare my judgments against them, for all their evil in forsaking me. They have made offerings to other gods and worshiped the works of their own hands. ¹⁷But you, dress yourself for work; arise, and say to them everything that I command you. Do not be dismayed by them, lest I dismay you before them. ¹⁸And I, behold, I make you this day a fortified city, an iron pillar, and bronze walls, against the whole land, against the kings of Judah, its officials, its priests, and the people of the land. ¹⁹They will fight against you, but they shall not prevail against you, for I am with you, declares the LORD, to deliver you."

Observing the Text

Who is speaking with God in this passage? What assignment has God given him (verse 5)?

____

____

____

What are the responsibilities of this assignment (verse 7)? What promise comes along with the task (verse 8)?

____

____

____

Whose words does a prophet speak (verse 9)?

____

____

____

Interpreting the Text

Why is God sending Jeremiah to preach against the people of Jerusalem?

____

____

____

What is Jeremiah's message to Judah? Try to summarize it in your own words.

____

____

____

How will the people and kings of Judah respond to the prophet's message? What would have been a better response?

____

____

____

Teaching

Most people think of a prophet as someone who is able to predict the future. In fact, a quick look in a thesaurus produces synonyms like forecaster, fortuneteller, seer, clairvoyant, and psychic. All these terms conjure up images of a mysterious figure with a crystal ball, warning people about future events in their lives.

However, the prophets in the Old Testament served a different purpose. They *were* often mysterious (and sometimes odd) figures, and they *did* announce the future at times. But, the primary role of a prophet was to speak for God. Their messages weren't limited to predicting future events, but included all the things that God would have them say to his covenant people. As authoritative spokesmen for God, they were primarily concerned with enforcing the covenant between God and the nation of Israel.

The Prophetic books are divided into two categories, Major and Minor, based not on the level of importance but on their length.

Major Prophets	Minor Prophets
Isaiah	Hosea
Jeremiah	Joel
Lamentations	Amos
Ezekiel	Obadiah
Daniel	Jonah
	Micah
	Nahum
	Habakkuk
	Zephaniah
	Haggai
	Zechariah
	Malachi

Think back to what we learned last week about the role of the Law in the Old Covenant. The Law listed the stipulations of the relationship between God and Israel. There were blessings for obedience (e.g. life, health, and agricultural abundance) and punishments for disobedience (e.g. death, disease, and destruction). Through his prophets, God graciously reminded Israel of their covenant with him. Rather than leaving his people to perish, God used the prophets to point out Israel's sin, warn of the imminent consequences of their unfaithfulness, and urge them to repent.

They used a variety of forms to deliver their divine messages including poetry, vivid metaphors, and allegories. At times God even commanded them to "act out" the prophecy to bring greater impact.[1] Prophets often

---

1 Hosea is commanded to marry a prostitute who is unfaithful to him to show Israel their unfaithfulness to God (Hosea 1:2). Ezekiel was told to build a small replica of Jerusalem

spoke using lawsuit language as a kind of prosecutor in a courtroom. They pronounced woes of destruction and proclaimed the promises of God. All of this was intended, first and foremost, for the audience of their own time.

Prophetic Perspective

The prophets did announce the future, but usually it was the immediate future of Israel, Judah, and the surrounding nations rather than our future. Most of the prophecies in the Old Testament found their fulfillment during the lifetime of the original hearers.

However, in the New Testament we read Jesus and others quoting Old Testament prophecy and applying it to Jesus and his contemporaries and even beyond. How can an Old Testament prophecy be fulfilled in the time of that prophet, in the time of Jesus, and again in the end times? And how are we to understand prophetic literature when one verse has already been fulfilled and the next verse has yet to be?

Imagine standing at a scenic overlook, gazing out over a mountain range. There are mountains as far as the eye can see. Varying in shape and shade, some are nearer than others, but from the perspective of the overlook our eyes have difficulty distinguishing the distances between the mountains before us. They look to be at a similar distance, but little does the viewer realize that these mountains are separated by many miles.

The future orientation of the prophet sees the fulfillment of his words in a similar way. The prophetic perspective opens the possibility that a prophecy can find dual fulfillment within and beyond the lifetime of the prophet. An example of this is found in the words of Isaiah to King Ahaz in Isaiah 7:14, *"Therefore the LORD himself will give you a sign. Behold, the virgin shall conceive and bear a son, and shall call his name Immanuel."*

---

under siege and then lay down on his left side for 390 days and then on his right side for 40 days to warn Israel of the number of years of punishment (Ezekiel 4).

Modern readers may well know that Matthew 1:22-23 applies the fulfillment of this prophecy to the birth of Jesus. However, scholars agree that this Immanuel figure also found immediate fulfillment within the lifetime of Ahaz. From Isaiah's perspective, he could see mountains for miles. He knew Immanuel would come in the future. How many miles separated the mountains in the foreground from the mountains in the background would only be seen when the ultimate Immanuel was born in Bethlehem over 700 years later. Let's look at some strategies to faithfully interpret the message of the prophets:

1. Some of the prophecies of the near future (for Israel) were set against the backdrop of the great, final future, and sometimes, they seem to blend together. Remember the prophetic perspective.

2. Prophets didn't always indicate intervals of time between events or chronological order. Attempts to use hindsight to map out a clear order of prophecy fulfillment may miss the point.

3. Many times when a prophet refers to future events he doesn't use the future tense.

4. The prophecy didn't always have to be fully understood by the prophet or the audience who heard the message. It may be explained and find its ultimate fulfillment later in an event in the New Testament, or it may still be waiting for fulfillment.

5. The role of the prophet was to challenge Israel's actions to match up with their beliefs, announcing the results of either choice.

Questions for Reflection

Before reading this lesson, what image did you have for a prophet? Has your thinking been challenged or rearranged in any way?

____

____

____

God sent the prophets to remind his people of the terms of his covenant with them. What does this action reveal to us about God's character? What are some similar ways that he reaches out to his people today?

____

____

____

Prayer

Ask God to give you an appreciation for the prophetic messages and his voice throughout redemptive history. Thank him that you have a Savior who fulfilled all the demands of the Old Covenant in your place.

SCRIPTURE MEMORY

For the word of God is living and active, sharper than any______________ ______, piercing to the division of soul and of spirit, of joints and of marrow, and discerning the__________and___ ________of the heart. —*Hebrews 4:12*

APOCALYPTIC LITERATURE

Scripture Study

Revelation 1:9-20

I, John, your brother and partner in the tribulation and the kingdom and the patient endurance that are in Jesus, was on the island called Patmos on account of the word of God and the testimony of Jesus. [10] I was in the Spirit on the Lord's day, and I heard behind me a loud voice like a trumpet [11] saying, "Write what you see in a book and send it to the seven churches, to Ephesus and to Smyrna and to Pergamum and to Thyatira and to Sardis and to Philadelphia and to Laodicea."

[12] Then I turned to see the voice that was speaking to me, and on turning I saw seven golden lampstands, [13] and in the midst of the lampstands one like a son of man, clothed with a long robe and with a golden sash around his chest. [14] The hairs of his head were white, like white wool, like snow. His eyes were like a flame of fire, [15] his feet were like burnished bronze, refined in a furnace, and his voice was like the roar of many waters. [16] In his right hand he held seven stars, from his mouth came a sharp two-edged sword, and his face was like the sun shining in full strength.

[17] When I saw him, I fell at his feet as though dead. But he laid his right hand on me, saying, "Fear not, I am the first and the last, [18] and the living one. I died, and behold I am alive forevermore, and I have the keys of Death and Hades. [19] Write therefore the things that you have seen, those that are and those that are to take place after this. [20] As for the mystery of the seven stars that you saw in my right hand, and the seven golden lampstands, the seven stars are the angels of the seven churches, and the seven lampstands are the seven churches.

Observing the Text

Who is writing? Where is he?

____

____

____

List the phrases that describe the physical appearance of the one who spoke to John.

____

____

____

What instruction does he give to John?

____

____

____

Interpreting the Text

Who is the one who speaks to John? What titles and accomplishments does he claim that could only be his (verses 17-18)?

____

____

____

What is John going to write about?

____

____

____

Read Daniel 10:1-12. Note any similarities you see between Daniel's and John's experiences. How would a familiarity with this passage have influenced the original audience of John's book?

____

____

____

Teaching

The apocalyptic genre of the Bible seems to draw some of the greatest interest. Perhaps it's the dragons, strange creatures, and epic battles that easily garners a following. While many might find the figures and images as entertaining as a modern apocalyptic movie about zombies and vampires, it's more likely that the intrigue stems from the interpretation (and often misinterpretation) of this genre.

Closely associated with prophetic literature, the apocalyptic writings use highly dramatic and symbolic material to describe events that often take place on a global scale. They are frequently narrated in the first-person as an eyewitness account, as is found in Revelation and Daniel.

How Apocalyptic Literature Differs from Prophecy:
1. Looks to God's movement not in history but to end history.
2. Predominantly presented in visions and dreams.
3. Images are often forms of fantasy.

Apocalyptic literature paints a picture of the end times. Students of the Bible are captivated by what it says about the final days of the world, and rightly so. But misguided methods for studying this type of literature has led some to over-analyze, over-hype, and over-predict current and future events. Let's examine some helpful tools to accurately hear from God in his apocalyptic literature.

Look for the author's own interpretation. When attempting to interpret this highly symbolic genre, we must always begin by searching for any clues or interpretations that the author himself provides elsewhere in the book. Before jumping to other books of the Bible, become familiar with images within the text you're studying. Often these images reappear in other chapters, and the author may even explain the meaning behind it. For example, Revelation 1:12 depicts seven golden lampstands later explained in verse 20 to be the seven churches addressed in the following chapters.

Understand the Old Testament background. Many of the images and ideas found in Revelation are taken from the Old Testament, particularly Ezekiel, Daniel, Zechariah, and Isaiah. In addition to being influenced by the persecution happening as it was written, Revelation draws on its readers' familiarity with these Old Testament apocalyptic works. This requires modern-day Bible students to rely on cross references, study notes, and commentaries to help them understand the connections that original readers would have naturally made due to their familiarity with the Old Testament.

Avoid over-interpreting every detail. See the vision as a whole. Not every number or detail "means" something. A detail may have been included to provide a more realistic or memorable description. For example, as Fee and Stuart point out, the sun turning black like sackcloth and stars falling like figs may simply make the whole vision of the earthquake in Revelation

6 more impressive, rather than symbolizing something specific.[1]

Remain cautiously open to the possibility of a secondary meaning, inspired by the Holy Spirit but not fully seen by the author or his readers. Once you do the work of studying the author's original intent, then (and only then) can you carefully consider secondary meanings that the author or his readers did not know. There's a chance that God sovereignly included images or figures that find their fulfillment years or even centuries after the canon of Scripture was closed. However, these secondary meanings must be cautiously and loosely held. History is filled with people who were convinced that everyone from the Pope to the President of the United States was the second beast (or Antichrist) described in Revelation 13. Be open to the possibility that God has a secondary meaning in mind, but also be open to the possibility that a guess of a second meaning is simply wrong.

Apocalyptic literature usually doesn't follow a strict chronology. Attempts to distill the recorded visions into a detailed order of future events will leave modern readers confused and frustrated. The message at the heart of this genre is God's control over history. He is sovereign over all future events, and all things that come to pass will ultimately result in him being glorified. Resist becoming too preoccupied with how and when these future events will unfold, and instead turn your attention to him who sovereignly works all things for his glory. Jesus said you won't be able to predict the day he returns, but you'll know it when he comes. Until then, worship him with all of your life.

Remember: When reading apocalyptic literature, we must understand that God's word to us is to be found first of all in God's word to the original audience.

---

1 Fee and Stuart, *How to Read the Bible for All Its Worth*, 256.

Questions for Reflection

Why do you think God included apocalyptic literature in the Bible? Why might he have kept it intentionally ambiguous and difficult to understand?

____

____

____

Do you struggle with anxiety or fear when you think about the end times? How do you think God wants us to respond to his promises about the future?

____

____

____

How can faith in God's sovereignty over history help to give us assurance about the future?

____

____

____

Prayer

Praise our God who holds the whole world's future in his hands. He is faithful, good, and worthy of our trust. Pray that we might study the end times with faith and assurance, rather than fear and anxiety.

SCRIPTURE MEMORY

______________________is living and active, sharper than any two-edged sword, piercing to the division of soul and of spirit, of______and of marrow, and discerning the thoughts and intentions__________. –*Hebrews 4:12*

POETRY AND WISDOM

Scripture Study

Proverbs 1:1-7

The proverbs of Solomon, son of David, king of Israel:

² To know wisdom and instruction,
to understand words of insight,

³ to receive instruction in wise dealing,
in righteousness, justice, and equity;

⁴ to give prudence to the simple,
knowledge and discretion to the youth—

⁵ Let the wise hear and increase in learning,
and the one who understands obtain guidance,

⁶ to understand a proverb and a saying,
the words of the wise and their riddles.

⁷ The fear of the LORD is the beginning of knowledge;
fools despise wisdom and instruction.

Observing the Text

Who is the author of this book?

____

____

____

Why is he writing? What would the original audience have hoped to gain from reading it?

____

____

____

What does he say is the starting point of knowledge?

____

____

____

Interpreting the Text

Read 1 Kings 3:3-12 and 4:29-34. How was Solomon uniquely qualified to write this passage?

____

____

____

What groups of people are listed in the Proverbs 1:1-7 as being able to benefit from Solomon's teaching? What benefit will each group gain? Who will not benefit?

____

____

____

Teaching

Biblical poetry is a unique genre. Not only are its verses primarily intended to be spoken or sung rather than read, but it's also often addressed to God or calling others to address God. While we mostly think of God's word as something that God says to us, this genre shows us that Scripture also encourages and even commands us to say something to God. Filled with imagery, symbols, metaphors, and other poetic devices, poetry appeals to the emotion. The book of Psalms is the chief example of poetry in the Bible, but it's not uncommon for someone to break out in song in the middle of a historical narrative (e.g. Deuteronomy 32; 2 Samuel 22; Luke 1:46-55).

Biblical poetry provides us with inspired examples of ways to honestly express ourselves to God. Psalms were generally placed into different categories depending on the occasion they would have been sung. There are psalms of lament, thanksgiving, praise, celebration, and trust. Poetry also expresses a range of emotion, including adoration, pain, longing, hope, joy, sadness, and even anger. This genre invites us to live reflectively and meditatively, deeply aware of the grace God has bestowed on us. For centuries, Christians have turned to Psalms and other biblical poetry to give them the words to speak when it's hard to find them themselves. Here are some keys to interpreting poetry effectively:

Poetry is usually addressed to the emotions. Look for the emotions being expressed in the text and ask yourself, "Do I feel what is taking place here?" Often the flow of the poem or song will move through multiple emotions. Seek to identify with the emotions expressed by the writer, and let it call you to express your authentic emotions to God.

Poetry follows certain rules and has its own literary techniques and structure. Unlike many contemporary poems and songs, the poetry in the

Bible doesn't rhyme in the original languages (or in the English translation). But it is filled with parallelism, metaphors, symbolism, hyperbole, and repetition. As you read, train yourself to be especially astute at recognizing parallelism; it's found in almost every poetic writing. With parallelism, two lines of poetry will say the same thing but in two different ways. Taken together, you'll have a better idea of what's being expressed. In Psalm 36:5, notice how the first two lines essentially say the same thing using different words.

> *Your steadfast love, O LORD, extends to the heavens,*
> *your faithfulness to the clouds.*

Poetry is not intended to teach specific doctrines. While of course poetry reflects doctrine, it should not be seen as a primary source for the exposition of doctrine. For example, David writes, "in sin did my mother conceive me" (Psalm 51:5). Fee and Stuart comment that this phrase is "hardly trying to establish the doctrine that conception is sinful, or that all conceptions are sinful, or that his mother was a sinner by getting pregnant, or that original sin applies to unborn children."[1] Instead, David's words are intended to express how pervasive his sin has been throughout all his life.

Wisdom Literature

Trafficking in the wisdom books of the Bible can provide valuable insight into godly living. This makes sense since wisdom is the ability to make good choices in life. However, readers should approach this genre with caution. An uninformed Bible student might easily misunderstand a text and therefore misapply it in a way that God did not intend.

Proverbs, Job, Ecclesiastes, and Song of Solomon are the primary books characterized as wisdom literature. Generally speaking, this is a broad

---

1 Fee and Stuart, *How to Read the Bible for All Its Worth*, 208.

category in which an older person with years of life experience relates wisdom to another. Thus, this type of literature tends to focus on behavior, making observations about everyday life.

The wisdom genre is most recognizable in the book of Proverbs. A proverb is a brief, particular expression of a truth. Its pithiness and brevity makes it memorable. By contrasting godly living and foolishness, they are meant to convey guidelines for living. Let's cover some methods that will help us get the most out of interpreting these nuggets of wisdom.

Proverbs are not promises. Like modern-day proverbs, biblical proverbs are not meant to spell out universal rules, nor do they promise a guaranteed outcome by following their advice. We know that in the modern proverb that "an apple a day" is not guaranteed to "keep the doctor away." Likewise, if you "train up a child in the way he should go," God does not promise that "even when he is old he will not depart from it" (Proverbs 22:6). Rather, Proverbs presents a wise course of life which makes the desired outcome more likely but not guaranteed.[2]

Proverbs often use figurative or hyperbolic language to make their point. Proverbs are similar in this sense to parables. They aren't always meant to be understood literally. Proverbs 18:6 warns, "A fool's lips walk into a fight, and his mouth invites a beating." It's clear that a fool's lips are not going to sprout legs and walk into a fight, but I bet we all know someone whose words have gotten them into trouble. Proverbs 22:16 says, "Whoever oppresses the poor to increase his own wealth, or gives to the rich, will only come to poverty." The point is to encourage generosity to the poor, rather than playing favorites for your own gain. If your rich neighbor knocks on the door asking for a cup of sugar, you don't have to slam the door in her face for fear of "giving to the rich."

---

2 Additional examples of proverbs often misunderstood to be promises include Proverbs 10:4; 16:3; 22:26-27.

Ask Yourself, "What behavior is being encouraged or discouraged?" Usually the meaning behind a proverb isn't too difficult to figure out when you look for the desired or discouraged choice. Proverbs 22:15 says, "Folly is bound up in the heart of a child, but the rod of discipline drives it far from him." The writer is not promoting child abuse, but rather encouraging parents to actively and lovingly correct their children. Proverbs 22:7, which says, "The rich rules over the poor, and the borrower is the slave of the lender," discourages (but does not prohibit) borrowing, because it places you at another's mercy until the debt is paid. Discerning what behavior is desirable or not will help us to see the verse's general principle for wise living.

Questions for Reflection

Is it ever difficult for you to express your feelings honestly in prayer? How could studying the Psalms help you to grow in that area?

What impact could studying biblical poetry have on the way you worship? In what ways can our corporate worship experiences reflect the richness and variation of the Psalms?

Why do you think it is common for someone to read Proverbs as promises rather than principles? How can we discern the difference between the two more precisely?

Prayer

Be grateful today for the Bible's wisdom to speak to our everyday feelings and experiences. God knows just what we need. Pray that we might seek understanding in his word where we find the road to abundant life.

WEEKLY EXERCISE

VARYING GENRES, VARYING APPROACHES

Look up the selected passages, identify the genre to which they belong, and put the principles in this week's lessons to work, interpreting them for believers today with a brief summary

Psalm 46:1-11

Literary Genre:

Summary Interpretation:

____

____

____

Revelation 21:22-27

Literary Genre:

Summary Interpretation:

____

____

____

Isaiah 52:1-7

Literary Genre:

Summary Interpretation:

____

____

____

Get Ready for Group

Write your memorized Scripture.

What observations and interpretations of Scripture were most meaningful to you?

Summarize your key takeaway(s) for this week.

What will you tell the group about the results of your exercise this week?

How has this week helped you better understand and apply the Spiritual Growth Grid?

____

____

____

____

____

09

STUDYING THE BIBLE (PART 5)

SCRIPTURE MEMORY

This Book of the Law shall not depart from your mouth, but you shall meditate on it day and night, so that you may be careful to do according to all that is written in it. For then you will make your way prosperous, and then you will have good success.

—Joshua 1:8

THE BIG IDEA

Scripture Study

James 1:22-25

But be doers of the word, and not hearers only, deceiving yourselves. [23] *For if anyone is a hearer of the word and not a doer, he is like a man who looks intently at his natural face in a mirror.* [24] *For he looks at himself and goes away and at once forgets what he was like.* [25] *But the one who looks into the perfect law, the law of liberty, and perseveres, being no hearer who forgets but a doer who acts, he will be blessed in his doing.*

Observing the Text

In verse 22, how is James saying that his readers would deceive themselves?

____

____

____

What does he want them to hear and do?

____

____

____

Interpreting the Text

What is James' main point in this passage? What does he want his reader to remember and act on?

____

____

____

Why is application essential to the Bible study process?

____

____

____

Teaching

You've made all your observations. You've studied the grammatical, historical, and literary context. You've consulted additional resources and looked up cross-references. Your notebook is filled with glorious insights and scratched-out heresy. Now it's time to take all that you've discovered and summarize it into a single statement that communicates the overall meaning behind the text. The final component of the interpretation step is to find the *Big Idea*. Don't skip this part.

Remember, in week 6 we learned that generally speaking, each text has only one interpretation. The author has one particular meaning he wants his readers to understand. That's the Big Idea. That's not to say your Big Idea statement must be exactly like someone else's, but they should at least be in the same ballpark.

The Big Idea statement has two parts: subject and complement.

The *subject* is the main question to which the author is responding. Thus, the subject should be stated as a question the author may have had in mind as he was writing. To arrive at the subject question, begin by asking yourself, "What is the author talking about? What question is he answering?"

Once you have that question written down, the *complement* is simply the answer that the text gives to that question. In both the subject and complement, try to use as much of the wording found in the passage as possible. The Big Idea then comes from joining the subject and complement together in the form of an affirmation, rather than a question. Let's look at an example using one of Jesus' shortest parables.

> *The kingdom of heaven is like treasure hidden in a field, which a man found and covered up. Then in his joy he goes and sells all that he has and buys that field.*
>
> Matthew 13:44

Subject: How should we respond to the good news of the kingdom of heaven?

Complement: By joyfully giving up all things in pursuit of the incomparable value of Jesus.

Big Idea: We should respond to the good news of the kingdom of heaven by joyfully giving up all things in pursuit of the incomparable value of Jesus.

Practice

What's the Big Idea of Hebrews 4:14-16? Refer back to your observations on page 127 and your interpretation on page 172-173.

> *Since then we have a great high priest who has passed through the heavens, Jesus, the Son of God, let us hold fast our confession. For we do not have a high priest who is unable to sympa-*

*thize with our weaknesses, but one who in every respect has
been tempted as we are, yet without sin. Let us then with confidence draw near to the throne of grace, that we may receive
mercy and find grace to help in time of need.*

Subject:

____

____

*(Remember to ask yourself, "What question is the writer of Hebrews
answering?" It should be stated as a question.)*

Complement:

____

____

____

(What answer does this text give to the question you wrote above?)

Big Idea:

____

____

____

(Combine the subject and complement into a complete sentence.)

Interpretation Recap

Before moving on to the final step in our study of the Bible, let's review the
interpretation process.

1. Let Scripture interpret Scripture.

The Bible is a complete, unified work written under the inspiration of God.
Thus, if in our study of a passage we read something that seems to contradict the rest of Scripture, it most likely means we haven't discovered the
correct meaning of that text. We ought to let the totality of God's revealed

word give insight into a particular text.

2. Utilize study tools to assist you in your correct interpretation.

Avoid turning to additional resources too early. Try to make your own observations and draw your own conclusions before holding them up to what gifted scholars might think. Go to God in prayer asking him to guide your thoughts and discoveries. When appropriate, consult some of the following resources:

- Different translations
- Study Bibles
- Concordance
- Cross References
- Bible Commentaries
- Bible Handbooks & Encyclopedias
- Bible Atlas/Maps
- Bible Dictionaries

3. Remember, a text cannot mean what it never meant!

The goal of the interpreter is to find the meaning the author intended for the original audience of the text. If you are the only one to have come to an interpretation that is different from how the church, after 2,000 years, has historically understood a text, you're probably the only one for a reason. Take a step back and try again.

Questions for Reflection

Was the practice difficult for you? Why do you think writing down the text's Big Idea is important?

____

____

____

Why is it important that our interpretation of a passage is harmonious with both the rest of Scripture and the church's historical understanding?

____

____

____

Prayer

Praise Jesus who became flesh to perfectly reflect God's ways to us and pay the price for our salvation with his death. Pray that we might explore Scripture with his wisdom, his knowledge, and his love.

SCRIPTURE MEMORY

This Book of the______shall not depart from your______, but you shall meditate on it day and night, so that you may be careful to do according to all that is______in it. For then you will make your way prosperous, and then you will have good______.

–Joshua 1:8

APPLICATION — WHY DOES IT MATTER?

Scripture Study

James 1:22-25

But be doers of the word, and not hearers only, deceiving yourselves.[23] For if anyone is a hearer of the word and not a doer, he is like a man who looks intently at his natural face in a mirror. [24] For he looks at himself and goes away and at once forgets what he was like. [25] But the one who looks into the perfect law, the law of liberty, and perseveres, being no hearer who forgets but a doer who acts, he will be blessed in his doing.

Observing the Text

What metaphor does James use to describe the one who hears the word but doesn't do it (verses 23-24)?

____

____

____

What contrasting verbs are found in these verses? Why is this contrast unexpected?

____

____

____

Interpreting the Text

What emotional response is James trying to incite with this metaphor?

____

____

____

What is James going to write about?

____

____

____

Why might someone study without pursuing life change? What does James say are the dangers there?

____

____

____

Teaching

You've made your observations by asking, "What does it say?" You've studied the context, used resources as needed, and interpreted the text by asking, "What does it *mean*?" You have your Big Idea statement. The final step of studying the Bible is *application*, where you ask, "Why does it *matter*?" Think of yourself like an engineer, taking an idea and making it work in real life. We must move from theory to practice.

After prayerfully poring over the text, you may find yourself mentally exhausted or merely satisfied with learning a new insight. You might even be tempted to skip this final step, thinking your work is over. Maybe you've learned something interesting that you didn't know before. Perhaps, you made a connection that you never noticed before. That's one of the great things about studying the Bible. But your work isn't done yet. Studying the Bible is not complete until the application is done. If needed, take a break before coming to the final step. Don't short-change application.

If we never apply the text to our lives, we will only have knowledge and won't see the life change that God desires for us. Our study of Scripture must move from our heads to our hearts to our hands. In fact, God commands us to apply his word to our lives: *"But be doers of the word, and not hearers only, deceiving yourselves"* (James 1:22). *"What you have learned and received and heard and seen in me—practice these things, and the God of peace will be with you"* (Philippians 4:9).

Identity Before Activity

As you seek to be "doers of the word" and to "practice these things," don't forget your activity ought to be a natural outflow of your gospel identity. Look back at Philippians 4:9. The things Paul commands us to practice are the things we have "learned and received and heard and seen." In other words, our behavior is a reflection of what we believe.[1]

Our application of the Bible should not focus on trying to do things in our own power. Rather, we trust in the power of Jesus and the working of the Spirit in our lives to bring about true gospel-centered life change. Does that include behavior? Does it include activity on our part? Of course it does, but our behavior is rooted in our beliefs.

---

1   For a refresher, review the concepts in week 6 of *An Introduction to Gospel-Centered Discipleship.*

Questions for Reflection

Why is it a temptation to quit studying when we finish interpretation? What are some reasons we might not spend time on application?

What does it look like when our Bible study doesn't move from our heads to our hearts to our hands? What dangers are there in accumulating knowledge without putting it to practice?

What happens when we emphasize behavior over beliefs?

Prayer

Thank God that he doesn't leave us on our own to try to muddle our way through life, without direction or understanding. He gives us his Son, his Spirit, and his Scriptures to guide us into the truly abundant life. Pray that his truth would transform our heads, hearts, and hands into the image of the one who made them all.

SCRIPTURE MEMORY

This Book of the Law shall not depart from your mouth, but you shall __________ on it day and night, so that you may be _______ to do __________ to all that is written in it. For then you will make your way __________, and then you will have good success.

—Joshua 1:8

APPLICATION – SPECK

Scripture Study

James 1:22-25

But be doers of the word, and not hearers only, deceiving yourselves.²³ For if anyone is a hearer of the word and not a doer, he is like a man who looks intently at his natural face in a mirror. ²⁴ For he looks at himself and goes away and at once forgets what he was like. ²⁵ But the one who looks into the perfect law, the law of liberty, and perseveres, being no hearer who forgets but a doer who acts, he will be blessed in his doing.

Observing the Text

Instead of *forgetting*, what is the hallmark of the one who not only hears but also acts? (verse 25)

____

____

____

What is the benefit of not only hearing, but doing what the word commands?

____

____

Interpreting the Text

How does James describe God's commands? Why should that be encouraging to us?

____

____

____

What does it look like when you study the Bible with a desire to let it transform your life? How might you respond to it differently with that purpose in place?

____

____

____

Teaching

One of the most widely used tools for applying the Bible is the SPECK method.[1] It's simply an acronym that provides a framework for how to put into practice what you've learned from a text. So, review your Big Idea and prayerfully reflect on the following ideas:

- **S – Sin to Confess or Avoid.** Did the Spirit convict you of any sin that you need to confess? Take the time to repent of sin to God and believe the good news of the gospel. How will you avoid any specific sins you were warned about in the text?

- **P – Promises to Claim.** Did God make a promise in the text that you can claim for yourself? How will you rest in this promise when you're tempted to trust in a source other than God?

---

1 The SPECK method has been so widely used by authors and teachers that the original source is unknown.

E - Examples to Follow. What godly behaviors are modeled in the text? What false beliefs do you have that cause you to behave differently? What truths do you need to believe instead? How will you follow this example for living this week?

C - Commands to Obey. What is God commanding you to do or stop doing? Do you find yourself wanting to obey this command or justifying disobedience? What false beliefs do you have that cause you to behave differently? What truths do you need to believe instead?

K – Knowledge about God. What new insights did you learn about who God is, what he did, who we are, or what we do? What response does this call for? How does this truth compel you to worship and adore God more?

You may or may not have something from all five categories for a given text. Perhaps you found a whole host of ways you can apply a text. Don't let that overwhelm you. Choose the one or two particular applications that seem to stand out most, then prayerfully consider how you might pursue greater faithfulness in them. You may find it helpful to write in a journal the specific actions you will take within a certain time period and who you will ask to help you. Consider writing a prayer expressing your trust that God will help you grow in this area.

Remember: You haven't finished until you've applied the truth you've learned.

Questions for Reflection

Why is it essential for any application methods to be carried out prayerfully? What is the danger of trying to change our behavior without the Spirit's leading?

____

____

____

Why would we need to be careful about choosing which promises of God to claim for ourselves? What are some ways in which people misuse or misapply biblical promises?

____

____

____

What happens to our application process when we stray from gospel centrality? In what ways are you tempted to focus on behavior without addressing belief?

____

____

____

Prayer

Pray that God would help you to identify the needed application of the Scriptures you study, clearly seeing both the message of the text and the needs of your heart. Thank him for the conviction the Spirit brings as evidence that you are his child, being conformed into the image of his Son.

WEEKLY EXERCISE

APPLICATION FOR HEBREWS 4:14-16

Let's practice application for Hebrews 4:14-16.

Big Idea:

____

____

____

S – Sin to Confess or Avoid

____

____

____

P – Promises to Claim

____

____

____

E - Examples to Follow

____

____

____

C - Commands to Obey

____

____

____

K – Knowledge about God

____

____

____

Choose the one or two particular applications that seem to stand out most, then prayerfully consider how you might pursue greater faithfulness in them. Write the specific actions you will take within a certain time period and who you will ask to help you.

Get Ready for Group

Write your memorized Scripture.

What observations and interpretations of Scripture were most meaningful to you?

Summarize your key takeaway(s) for this week.

What will you tell the group about the results of your exercise this week?

How has this week helped you better understand and apply the Spiritual Growth Grid?

____

____

____

____

____

10

HEARING GOD'S VOICE IN PRAYER (PART 1)

SCRIPTURE MEMORY

This Book of the Law shall not depart from your mouth, but you shall meditate on it day and night, so that you may be careful to do according to all that is written in it. For then you will make your way prosperous, and then you will have good success.

—Joshua 1:8

THE POSTURE OF PRAYER

Scripture Study

Matthew 6:5-13

And when you pray, you must not be like the hypocrites. For they love to stand and pray in the synagogues and at the street corners, that they may be seen by others. Truly, I say to you, they have received their reward. 6 But when you pray, go into your room and shut the door and pray to your Father who is in secret. And your Father who sees in secret will reward you.

7 And when you pray, do not heap up empty phrases as the Gentiles do, for they think that they will be heard for their many words. 8 Do not be like them, for your Father knows what you need before you ask him. 9 Pray then like this:

Our Father in heaven,
hallowed be your name.
10 Your kingdom come,
your will be done,
on earth as it is in heaven.

11 Give us this day our daily bread,

12 and forgive us our debts,

   as we also have forgiven our debtors.

13 And lead us not into temptation,

   but deliver us from evil.

Observing the Text (verses 5-6)

In verse 5, who are we told not to pray like? How do they pray?

____

____

____

Why do they pray in this way?

____

____

____

According to verse 6, how are we told to pray?

____

____

____

Interpreting the Text (verses 5-6)

What is the "reward" that the hypocrites receive and why is this reward not the goal of prayer?

____

____

____

Is Jesus telling us in verse 5 that we should never pray in public and can only pray in private? Why or why not?

____

____

____

What does the posture/location of our body in verse 6 tell us about what the posture/location of our heart should be in prayer?

____

____

____

Teaching

God's primary way of speaking today is through his word, but as we discussed in Week 2, there are other ways that God speaks today. Over the next two weeks, we're going to focus on hearing God's voice through prayer. While we mostly think of prayer as an exercise in speaking and not listening, God's desire for our prayer life is less like a monologue and more like a dialogue. Through prayer, we speak to God and God speaks to us.

As we pray, we tune our hearts to hear from God. We silence the noise of our lives so we might become more sensitive to the voice of God. We may not hear God's literal audible voice, but the Holy Spirit may lead us in a new way, confirm a certain direction, or impress on us someone to pray for. Also, when we fill our hearts and minds with Scripture through study and memorization, sometimes in prayer the Spirit will bring to mind a passage or truth that he wants us to apply.

Our posture matters. We come to God in prayer in a posture of humility. It's a spiritual posture, not necessarily a physical one, although a physically humble posture can be a helpful reminder for us of the humility faith requires. That's why most of us associate bowing our heads, closing our eyes, and clasping our hands as a position for prayer. Add kneeling to that, and it's difficult not to be mindful of our spiritual posture before God.

It's worth noting that the Bible doesn't say you have to kneel to pray. In fact, the Bible rarely speaks of people kneeling to pray. But often our physical posture reflects our attitude in prayer. We might ask ourselves which attitude our physical posture more often demonstrates: humility or hurry. If we find ourselves mostly or exclusively praying on the run (e.g. while driving, showering, or exercising), perhaps we have an attitude problem. Taking the time to stop, find a quiet place, and kneel before God requires us to slow down and posture our hearts as if it does not all depend on us.

Think of prayer like communication in any other relationship. You may send your spouse or a close friend text messages throughout the day. They could be messages expressing your appreciation and care for them. They could be questions or requests for things you'd like them to do. Text messages are a great way to stay in contact throughout the day, but if you never actually have a sit-down, face-to-face conversation with them, there's an issue there. Making time for regular, intentional conversation is essential in a healthy relationship.

Prayer is the same way. Yes, you should pray on the go. But do not neglect devoting yourself to a regular time of prayer with a physical posture that reflects a spiritual posture of humility and faith. Humility is a sober condition in which one sees the world accurately. By praying we aren't just trying to get things from God, rather, we are aligning our hearts to God's so that we might live with an accurate perception of the universe. People of prayer are reminded regularly that God is in control, and we are not. God is the provider, and we are not. God is God, and we are not.

Jesus taught a way of life that cultivates humility. As part of that, he called us to daily — even unceasing — prayer. For the next two weeks, we will study the Model Prayer in Matthew 6 in order to learn from Jesus how we are to pray. Make it your goal to grow your personal prayer life over the next two weeks as you study Jesus' "how-to" instructions. If you will commit yourself to follow this simple model, you can develop a prayer life that is sustainable and life-giving, and you will discover through prayer that you can hear God's voice.

Questions for Reflection

What are your current prayer habits? When and how do you regularly pray?

____

____

____

Is your prayer more like a monologue or dialogue? Does your posture demonstrate humility or hurry? What changes would you like to see happen in your personal prayer life?

____

____

____

How have you experienced a closer alignment of your heart with God's as you pray? How have you felt a lack of alignment when your habits of prayer haven't continued?

____

____

____

Prayer

Thank God for making a way for us to speak to him in prayer through the blood of his Son. Pray that you would grow in humility as you consider his beauty and holiness, gaining a deeper appreciation for his grace extended to us despite our sin.

SCRIPTURE MEMORY

This Book of the Law shall not depart_______________, but you shall meditate on it ____________, so that you may be careful to do according to________________in it. For then you will make your way prosperous, and then______________________.

—Joshua 1:8

PRAYING WITH A MODEL

Scripture Study

Matthew 6:5-13

And when you pray, you must not be like the hypocrites. For they love to stand and pray in the synagogues and at the street corners, that they may be seen by others. Truly, I say to you, they have received their reward. [6] But when you pray, go into your room and shut the door and pray to your Father who is in secret. And your Father who sees in secret will reward you.

[7] And when you pray, do not heap up empty phrases as the Gentiles do, for they think that they will be heard for their many words. [8] Do not be like them, for your Father knows what you need before you ask him. [9] Pray then like this:

Our Father in heaven,
hallowed be your name.
[10] Your kingdom come,
your will be done,
on earth as it is in heaven.

11 Give us this day our daily bread,

12 and forgive us our debts,

as we also have forgiven our debtors.

13 And lead us not into temptation,

but deliver us from evil.

Observing the Text (verses 7-8)

In verse 7, who are we told not to pray like? How do they pray?

Why do they pray in this way?

According to verse 8, is there anything we can request of God that he does not already know?

Interpreting the Text (verses 7-8)

What do you think Jesus means by "empty phrases"? Can you think of some examples?

Does "do not heap up empty phrases" mean that we can never repeat ourselves when we pray? What's the difference??

____

____

____

Write down all the reasons you can think of for why we should still pray, even though our "Father knows what you need before you ask" (verse 8).

____

____

____

Teaching

Jesus' disciples had seen many people pray throughout their lives. They grew up going to the Jewish synagogue or temple and reciting prayers. But when they saw and heard Jesus pray, something was different. He prayed in a way that intrigued them. His prayers were more intimate, not just memorized words emanating from the deep recesses of the mind rather than the heart. There was something about the way Jesus prayed that made the disciples want to learn to pray like him.

Jesus taught them what is sometimes called the Lord's Prayer. A better descriptor might be the Model Prayer, because Jesus presents it less like a prayer to recite (although Christians have for centuries), and more like a guide to follow. When you pray according to the Model Prayer you will know that, no matter what you are praying about, you are praying according to Jesus' pattern.

In Matthew 6:5-13, Jesus begins with a valuable lesson about the heart of prayer. The eloquence or number of words isn't what's important. Instead, the content of the prayer is what matters. The words you pray should come from your heart and be directed to God. Some people in Jesus' day were evidently in the habit of speaking lengthy prayers, because they thought God would be more likely hear them or that others would be impressed by how "spiritual" they sounded. But trying to impress God with your colorful vocabulary is futile. Likewise, trying to impress others misses the point. In verse 7, Jesus calls these "empty phrases." How would you like God to refer to something you prayed as an empty phrase?

Jesus then reminds his disciples that God is already aware of what's going on with us. We can skip all the fancy phrases and "spiritual" jargon, and speak to God with simple honesty. But this brings up a really important question: If God already knows what I need, why do I need to pray? That is a great question about the purpose of prayer. We don't pray in order to inform God of what we need or to show him something that has escaped his attention. You are not filling God in on information that he doesn't know, as if you are adding to his knowledge. That would mean God is changed by our prayers.

Instead, when you pray you are going to God and proclaiming your belief that he is God, that he knows and cares, and that he has the power to work in your life. Prayer does not change God. Rather, prayer changes us. That's at least one way prayer is a dialogue and not a monologue. Through the inner-working of the Spirit, God speaks, transforming us by his voice. Through prayer our faith grows, our will is aligned to his, and our hearts worship him in response to his unchanging nature. The Model Prayer provides a pattern to speak with our Father who already knows what we need.

Pray then like this:
Our Father in heaven,
hallowed be your name.
Your kingdom come,
your will be done,
on earth as it is in heaven.
Give us this day our daily bread,
and forgive us our debts,
as we also have forgiven our debtors.
And lead us not into temptation,
but deliver us from evil.

Questions for Reflection

How do you feel about praying aloud in front of others? What are the dangers of doing so? What benefits are there to praying aloud in a group?

____

____

____

Have you ever felt like you need just the right words to be heard by God? Have you ever neglected to pray because you felt intimidated or uncertain?

____

____

____

How might it impact our prayers if we recognize that God is already aware of our needs, fears and hurts? How might it impact your relationship with him?

____

____

____

Prayer

Praise the God who we don't have to strive to impress in any way, who loved us when we were his enemies, and who is bringing about our transformation into his Son's image. Thank him for the assurance that he knows us in every way and wants us to bring it all before his throne in prayer.

SCRIPTURE MEMORY

_________________________shall not de-

part from your mouth, but you shall

meditate on it day and night, so that

_________________to do according

to all that is written in it. ________

_____________your way prosperous,

and then you will have___________.

—_Joshua 1:8_

OUR FATHER IN HEAVEN, HALLOWED BE YOUR NAME

Scripture Study

Matthew 6:5-13

And when you pray, you must not be like the hypocrites. For they love to stand and pray in the synagogues and at the street corners, that they may be seen by others. Truly, I say to you, they have received their reward. ⁶ But when you pray, go into your room and shut the door and pray to your Father who is in secret. And your Father who sees in secret will reward you.

⁷ And when you pray, do not heap up empty phrases as the Gentiles do, for they think that they will be heard for their many words. ⁸ Do not be like them, for your Father knows what you need before you ask him.⁹ Pray then like this:

Our Father in heaven,
hallowed be your name.
¹⁰ Your kingdom come,

your will be done,

   on earth as it is in heaven.

[11] Give us this day our daily bread,

[12] and forgive us our debts,

   as we also have forgiven our debtors.

[13] And lead us not into temptation,

   but deliver us from evil.

Observing the Text (verse 9)

In verse 9, who is the prayer directed toward (what name is specifically mentioned)?

____

____

____

Does this prayer start with God or with us?

____

____

____

Interpreting the Text (verse 9)

Does "pray then like this" mean we should repeat this exact prayer or that we should use this prayer as a guideline? Or are we free to do either?

____

____

____

How would you explain the meaning of "hallowed be your name" in your own words?

____

____

____

Why do you think this prayer starts with acknowledging God's holiness?

____

____

____

Teaching

You can tell a lot about two people's relationship just by the way they address each other. For instance, someone might call their spouse "baby," "darling," "sugar," or "honey." These names indicate a deep, intimate relationship between two people. But if you meet someone for the first time, maybe a customer or a new boss, and you say, *"Hello, sugar!"* you are probably going to have to deal with a weird look. How we address someone is directly tied to the closeness of our relationship with them. The less we know someone, the more formally we address them. The more we know someone, the more intimately we address them.

In Matthew 6:9, Jesus instructs us to address God as *Father.* God invites us into an intimate connection with him, pictured as a father-child relationship. Remember the Spiritual Growth Grid:

*God is our **father** who has **adopted** us as members of his **family** who **love and serve** one another.*

In Jesus' day, Jews never dared to call God Father. In fact, the Old Testament contains no examples of a Jewish person addressing God directly as Father.[1] But through Jesus, there's a new way to relate to God. Galatians 4:4-7 explains this new relationship made possible through Christ.

---

1 Sproul, R.C. "What does it mean for us to call God our Father?" Ligonier Ministries, www.ligonier.org/learn/qas/what-does-it-mean-us-call-god-our-father.

But when the fullness of time had come, God sent forth his Son, born of woman, born under the law, to redeem those who were under the law, so that we might receive adoption as sons. And because you are sons, God has sent the Spirit of his Son into our hearts, crying, "Abba! Father!" So you are no longer a slave, but a son, and if a son, then an heir through God.

When you become a follower of Jesus, your heart cries out "Abba! Father!" which is what children would have called their fathers in that day. It's an intimate and personal title, something like calling God "dearest father." You are adopted into God's family. He is your Father, and you are his child who is afforded all the power, privilege, and protection that title entails. The ability to address God as Father is an amazing gift!

However, addressing God as Father doesn't seem amazing for some. Because of their relationship with their earthly father, this is a less-than-flattering description for God. For them, it's like calling God a four-letter word. Bad earthly fathers can be silent, violent, or simply absent, making it difficult to allow God to redeem and redefine what a good father is really like.

Nevertheless, it's worth noting that God's fatherhood blows all earthly fathers out of the water. Some people grew up with a great father. Some grew up with a terrible father. God is a better Father than all of them. He loves you more, provides for you more, and protects you more. He's the perfect Father. He's not moody or grouchy in the morning. God loves you the same on your good days as he does on your bad days.

Hallowed Be Your Name
The first sentence of Jesus' Model Prayer underscores the most essential ingredients in our relationship with God and in our prayers: he is our Father, and we acknowledge that his name should be hallowed. To hallow means to honor or revere as holy. It is a plea, asking God to cause his name

to be known and for him to be worshipped as Lord in our hearts and in the hearts of all people.

When we pray, we come before the Almighty Creator of heaven and earth. By his power he sustains all creation. When we ask in prayer that God's name would be hallowed, we merely acknowledge what is eternally true: God is supremely holy, supremely valued, and worthy of all praise. There is no one like him.

> *I am God, and there is none like me,*
> *declaring the end from the beginning*
>   *and from ancient times things not yet done,*
> *saying, "My counsel shall stand,*
>   *and I will accomplish all my purpose,"*
> *calling a bird of prey from the east,*
>   *the man of my counsel from a far country.*
> *I have spoken, and I will bring it to pass;*
>   *I have purposed, and I will do it.*

Isaiah 46:9-11

Questions for Reflection

Describe your relationship with your earthly father. How has that affected or changed your perception of God as Father?

____

____

____

When you read Galatians 4:4-7, what benefits do you see of being adopted into God's family?

____

____

____

What would it mean for God's name to be hallowed in every area of your life?

____

____

____

Prayer

Praise God the Father who loves you, remembering his unfailing devotion to his children. Ask him to be honored today in your heart, life, and home by your obedience and worship.

WEEKLY EXERCISE

PRAYING SCRIPTURE

Praying the Bible back to God can be a helpful way to guide your prayers. You can do this with any passage, but praying through the Psalms is the easiest way to start since they are written as songs or prayers designed to be sung or recited to God. Simply reading a Psalm is a form of prayer. But you can get creative with it too. There is no formula for how that looks, but you might start by reading a line from the Psalm and then praying something similar in your own words. You can pray line by line through a whole Psalm this way.

For example, Psalm 46:1 says, "God is our refuge and strength, a very present help in trouble." You might pray something like: Father, you are my source of peace and power. I repent of times when I try to live in my own strength. Thank you for your faithful presence. I need you to be my strength today as I face a tough situation at work. I trust you today to be my refuge and strength.

Pray through Psalm 130.

Out of the depths I cry to you, O LORD!
2 O LORD, hear my voice!
Let your ears be attentive
    to the voice of my pleas for mercy!
3 If you, O LORD, should mark iniquities,
    O LORD, who could stand?
4 But with you there is forgiveness,
    that you may be feared.
5 I wait for the LORD, my soul waits,
    and in his word I hope;
6 my soul waits for the LORD
    more than watchmen for the morning,
    more than watchmen for the morning.
7 O Israel, hope in the LORD!

For with the LORD there is steadfast love,
and with him is plentiful redemption.
8 And he will redeem Israel
from all his iniquities.

278

Get Ready for Group

Write your memorized Scripture.

What observations and interpretations of Scripture were most meaningful to you?

Summarize your key takeaway(s) for this week.

What will you tell the group about the results of your exercise this week?

How has this week helped you better understand and apply the Spiritual Growth Grid?

____

____

____

____

____

11

HEARING GOD'S VOICE IN PRAYER (PART 2)

SCRIPTURE MEMORY

When the Spirit of truth comes, he will guide you into all the truth, for he will not speak on his own authority, but whatever he hears he will speak, and he will declare to you the things that are to come. *—John 16:13*

YOUR KINGDOM COME, YOUR WILL BE DONE

Scripture Study

Matthew 6:5-13

And when you pray, you must not be like the hypocrites. For they love to stand and pray in the synagogues and at the street corners, that they may be seen by others. Truly, I say to you, they have received their reward. ⁶ But when you pray, go into your room and shut the door and pray to your Father who is in secret. And your Father who sees in secret will reward you.

⁷ And when you pray, do not heap up empty phrases as the Gentiles do, for they think that they will be heard for their many words. ⁸ Do not be like them, for your Father knows what you need before you ask him. ⁹ Pray then like this:

Our Father in heaven,
hallowed be your name.
¹⁰ Your kingdom come,
your will be done,
on earth as it is in heaven.

¹¹ Give us this day our daily bread,

¹² and forgive us our debts,

   as we also have forgiven our debtors.

¹³ And lead us not into temptation,

   but deliver us from evil.

Observing the Text (verse 10)

What are we asking for when we pray verse 10?

____

____

____

What does "your kingdom" refer to? (HINT: see Mark 1:15)

____

____

____

How are earth and heaven contrasted?

____

____

____

Interpreting the Text (verse 10)

What are we acknowledging about God's character when we pray "Your kingdom come, your will be done, on earth as it is in heaven"?

____

____

____

What would it look like for God's will to be done here in the same way it is done in heaven? How might that affect your daily choices or your attitude toward your circumstances?

____

____

____

In what ways do our prayers often reveal that we are praying "my kingdom come" rather than "your kingdom come"?

____

____

____

Teaching

Verse 10 of the Model Prayer takes our relationship with the Father a step further: *"Your kingdom come, your will be done, on earth as it is in heaven."* By praying this, we not only acknowledge God as God, but we confess our belief that his will should be done here in our life. Jesus is teaching us that we can be confident that God is inclined to bless us, and that truth should be reflected in the way we pray. The bedrock on which prayer is built is the belief that God's will being done is the very best thing that could happen to us because he is God, he loves us, and he knows the best for us.

But what exactly are we asking for? We are taught to pray that God's kingdom would come. What is the kingdom of God? Graeme Goldsworthy defines the kingdom of God as "God's people in God's place under God's rule."[1] In other words, it's about the people and the place where God is King. Certainly that is the case in heaven, as Jesus says. God rules

---

1 Graeme Goldsworthy, *Gospel and Kingdom* (Crownhill: Paternoster Press, 1981), 54-55.

in heaven. His will is done perfectly there. Where God's will is done is where his kingdom has come. This prayer is that God's kingdom would be expanded beyond the heavenly realm and his will would be done on earth. In one sense, this is a prayer for the imminent second return of Jesus. When Christ comes again to earth, the kingdom of God will be on earth. From that day forward, his will shall most certainly be done on earth as it is in heaven. In another sense, this prayer is for God's kingdom and will to be established in the world today. It's a prayer that the gospel would take root in and transform whole societies as well as our hearts.

Surrender Your Will

These words are a prayer of surrender to God's control. The kingdom comes when Jesus becomes King of your life. When we follow Jesus' Model Prayer, we say, *"God, I honor you as God and want to experience your will being done in my life today, just as those in heaven experience it."* Those words speak volumes about your relationship with God, implying that you believe God's words, you trust God's ways, and you want his will to be the directing power in your life.

This study has been focused on hearing God's voice, which is another way of saying discovering God's will. When we pray this prayer, we are committing ourselves to continually seek to hear from God and asking him to align our hearts with his will. We are asking God to change us. In seeking for God's will to be done in our lives, we are submitting ourselves to what he says and reorienting all of our thoughts, beliefs, and behaviors to be in accordance with his desire for our lives. We are saying, *"Because you are my King who called me to be your citizen, I will listen and obey when you speak."*

That's a big prayer! Everyone has an opinion, and everyone has a will. Think about your money. You and your family, all the people in your life, advertisers, and even your dog all have a will for how you should use your money. Everyone else seeks to influence your will in some way. This prayer is about saying, *"God's will wins every time. There is no debate or competition. All my money belongs to God. I want what he wants."* This prayer determines that God's will is the dominant and liberating will in your life. That's a really big prayer!

Questions for Reflection

Can you confidently pray to God and tell him you are ready to accept his will for you? If not, why?

____

____

____

What part of your life do you struggle to submit to God's will (For example, money, time, relationships, sexual ethic, career, kids, future plans, or possessions)? Why is that a struggle?

____

____

____

How can you grow this week in hearing from God so you can know his will?

____

____

____

Prayer

Pray, like Jesus did, that your kingdom would fade in order to establish his. Pray, like Jesus did, that your will would be aligned with the will of your King and that you may readily carry out his commands when you hear his voice.

SCRIPTURE MEMORY

When the______of truth comes, he will guide you into all the truth, for he will not speak on his own authority, but whatever he______he will ____, and he will declare to you the things that are to come. —*John 16:13*

GIVE US THIS DAY OUR DAILY BREAD

Scripture Study

Matthew 6:5-13

And when you pray, you must not be like the hypocrites. For they love to stand and pray in the synagogues and at the street corners, that they may be seen by others. Truly, I say to you, they have received their reward. ⁶ But when you pray, go into your room and shut the door and pray to your Father who is in secret. And your Father who sees in secret will reward you.

⁷ And when you pray, do not heap up empty phrases as the Gentiles do, for they think that they will be heard for their many words. ⁸ Do not be like them, for your Father knows what you need before you ask him.⁹ Pray then like this:

Our Father in heaven,
hallowed be your name.
¹⁰ Your kingdom come,
your will be done,
on earth as it is in heaven.

> *¹¹ Give us this day our daily bread,*
>
> > *¹² and forgive us our debts,*
> >
> > > *as we also have forgiven our debtors.*
> >
> > *¹³ And lead us not into temptation,*
> >
> > > *but deliver us from evil.*

Observing the Text (verse 11)

What are we instructed to ask for in this prayer?

____

____

____

How often should we pray this prayer? Why?

____

____

____

Interpreting the Text (verse 11)

Notice the structure of the prayer. Verses 9-10 start with God. Verses 11-13 then lead into our needs. What does this say about how we should structure our prayer?

____

____

____

Why should our focus first be on God when we pray?

____

____

____

What types of things could be included in our "daily bread"?

____

____

____

Teaching

_____

"Will you help me?" "Will you marry me?" "Would you consider me for this job?" Many things change in our lives when we ask. Asking is a fundamental part of prayer, and Jesus teaches us to ask God daily for what we need. He says "Give us this day our daily bread." Bread obviously means food, but it also represents all we need for life. Jesus teaches us to ask God for what we need. Here are four reasons why it is important that we ask God daily.

1. *When you develop a habit of asking, you cultivate a dependence on him.* Asking God is simply recognizing that you need someone more capable than yourself to provide what you need for life. Asking God is an admission that you can't do it yourself and you trust him to help. God wants us to live in dependence on him. Perhaps you can adopt this tongue-in-cheek prayer: *"Dear God, so far today, I am doing alright. I have not gossiped, lost my temper, been greedy, grumpy, nasty, selfish, or self-indulgent. I have not whined, cursed, or eaten any chocolate. However, I am going to get out of bed in a few minutes, and I will need a lot more help after that."*

2. *When you ask God, you acknowledge him as your source.* We proclaim that God is good, and out of his goodness to us he can choose when and how he will provide, even if it's not in the way we thought he would. One reason we don't ask God is our pride. We think, *I've got this. I don't need God's help for this one.* God wants you to see him as the source for all your needs. Asking moves our heart toward

humility. Our default mode is self-centeredness and self-sufficiency.

3. *Asking God helps us avoid worry.* For those of us who struggle with control issues, this seems to contradict the first two points. We think, *If I'm depending on God as my only source of provision, how can I not worry?* We're used to being in control, and when we're not, we get worried. This prayer calls us to let God hold the future. We can plan and prepare without worry because we know that we don't have the capacity to control the future. We let God be in charge of that. The Model Prayer says "Give us *today* our daily bread." We rely on God for what we need today and let God take care of tomorrow.

4. *Asking God helps mold our value system.* If a child is given complete freedom to eat whatever they want for dinner, they would choose candy or ice cream or something else filled with sugar. That's why it's not up to them. When it comes to providing food for children, part of a parent's role is to help children make healthy choices rather than just giving them whatever they want. Prayer is similar. If it were up to us, we would always want more and more comfort, ease, and success. Asking God for what we need invites him to have a say in what we need and want. We are submitting our desires to him and asking if they are consistent with his. Over time, we find that our desires gradually change. More and more, we will find that our prayer is "not my will, but yours, be done" (Luke 22:42).

Asking God has as much to do with shaping our character as filling our plates. When we ask God, we acknowledge our dependence on him and our willingness to accept his response. When we ask God, we declare that we receive his forgiveness for our guilt and know he loves us and is inclined to bless us even though we've sinned. When we ask God we acknowledge that God can change things, and most of all, he can change us.

Questions for Reflection

Have you ever been hesitant or afraid to ask God for something? Why?

____

____

____

When you want something, is your first inclination to take control or to pray? What does that say about your dependence on God?

____

____

____

How are your values reflected in what you ask God?

____

____

____

Prayer

Pray, like Jesus did, that God would provide all that you need for today. Maybe you need rest, nourishment, strength, grace, protection, comfort, patience, guidance, or peace. Thank him for his care that covers you every moment, bringing about his perfect plan for your life.

SCRIPTURE MEMORY

When the______________comes, he will guide you into all the_____, for he will not speak on his own authority, but whatever he hears he will speak, and he will______ to you the things that are to come. —*John 16:13*

FORGIVE US
OUR DEBTS

Scripture Study

Matthew 6:5-13

And when you pray, you must not be like the hypocrites. For they love to stand and pray in the synagogues and at the street corners, that they may be seen by others. Truly, I say to you, they have received their reward. ⁶ But when you pray, go into your room and shut the door and pray to your Father who is in secret. And your Father who sees in secret will reward you.

⁷ And when you pray, do not heap up empty phrases as the Gentiles do, for they think that they will be heard for their many words. ⁸ Do not be like them, for your Father knows what you need before you ask him.⁹ Pray then like this:

> *Our Father in heaven,*
> *hallowed be your name.*
> *¹⁰ Your kingdom come,*
> *your will be done,*
> *on earth as it is in heaven.*

> *11 Give us this day our daily bread,*
>
> *12 and forgive us our debts,*
>
> *as we also have forgiven our debtors.*
>
> *13 And lead us not into temptation,*
>
> *but deliver us from evil.*

Observing the Text (verses 12-13)

In order to ask God to forgive us, what does verse 12 say we must do?

____

____

____

According to verse 13, whose strength must we rely on to conquer evil in this world?

____

____

____

Interpreting the Text (verses 12-13)

Why do you think that asking for forgiveness is such an important part of praying?

____

____

____

How is God's forgiveness of us related to our forgiveness of others? (see also Matthew 6:14-15)

____

____

____

Why do we need to ask God for help in avoiding temptation and evil?

____

____

____

Teaching

"Just watch me and do it the way I do it." Have you ever given those instructions to someone? You would only say those words if you were confident in your ability to do something well and certain that another person could learn by following your lead. A key part of prayer is asking God to forgive us. In the Model Prayer, Jesus instructs us confess our sin and to ask God to forgive the moral debt that sin accumulates. Our sin has piled up a moral debt to God that we cannot repay. When we ask God to forgive us, by faith in Jesus, we appeal to his grace to erase our moral debt. And he does! Confessing our sin affirms our acceptance of Jesus' death on the cross as payment for our debt. It's a reminder of our need for a savior and his grace to provide one.

There is another aspect of asking for forgiveness mentioned in this prayer. Jesus instructs us to ask God to forgive our debts "as we have also forgiven our debtors." Jesus says we should be ready to forgive other people who have sinned against us to the same extent that we want God to be ready to forgive our debt with him. Our prayers for forgiveness take on a character-shaping request for God's help. In the Model Prayer, we ask God for mercy and forgiveness while also asking him to make our character like his, so we can extend that same mercy and forgiveness to other people.

If we do not ask God to forgive us and receive his forgiveness, our guilt will keep us from having a healthy, joyful relationship with God. And if we won't forgive others, we will build up resentment in our souls that will destroy us. Keeping track of how other people hurt us, carrying a grudge, and reminding people of their sins is the exact opposite of how we want God to treat us and the exact opposite of how God does treat us.

Jesus shows us in the Model Prayer that we should ask God not only to forgive our debts but also to infuse us with his own forgiving, life-giving character. Ask God to make forgiveness something that both comes to you from him and passes through you to other people.

Questions for Reflection

Is there anyone in your life you have not forgiven for something they have done to you? How do you think God would respond to you if he treated your mistakes the way you have treated theirs?

____

____

____

What steps of forgiveness do you need to take? How could you extend God's grace to other people by forgiving them?

____

____

____

When is the last time you prayed with another person about things that are temptations to you? What positive impacts might there be?

____

____

____

Prayer

Take some time to confess your sin to God. Pray that any sins that have disrupted your relationship with him are completely forgiven. Thank God for the strength, courage, and love to extend grace to others from the grace that we have been given.

WEEKLY EXERCISE

WRITING A PRAYER

When praying, many people find themselves easily distracted and before they know it, their mind is wandering. They begin praying about a situation going on in their life, but soon start thinking about everything they have to do that day or things they need to get from the grocery store. A helpful way to focus your mind is to write out your prayer.

Use the space below or a journal to write a prayer.

Get Ready for Group

Write your memorized Scripture.

What observations and interpretations of Scripture were most meaningful to you?

Summarize your key takeaway(s) for this week.

What will you tell the group about the results of your exercise this week?

How has this week helped you better understand and apply the Spiritual Growth Grid?

____

____

____

____

____

12

PROPHECY, PROMPTINGS AND PEOPLE

SCRIPTURE MEMORY

When the Spirit of truth comes, he will guide you into all the truth, for he will not speak on his own authority, but whatever he hears he will speak, and he will declare to you the things that are to come. —*John 16:13*

SCRIP

When the S

will guide y

OTHER WAYS
GOD SPEAKS

Scripture Study

John 14:15-31

If you love me, you will keep my commandments. [16] And I will ask the Father, and he will give you another Helper, to be with you forever, [17] even the Spirit of truth, whom the world cannot receive, because it neither sees him nor knows him. You know him, for he dwells with you and will be in you.

[18] I will not leave you as orphans; I will come to you. [19] Yet a little while and the world will see me no more, but you will see me. Because I live, you also will live. [20] In that day you will know that I am in my Father, and you in me, and I in you. [21] Whoever has my commandments and keeps them, he it is who loves me. And he who loves me will be loved by my Father, and I will love him and manifest myself to him." [22] Judas (not Iscariot) said to him, "Lord, how is it that you will manifest yourself to us, and not to the world?" [23] Jesus answered him, "If anyone loves me, he will keep my word, and my Father will love him, and we will come to him and make our home with him. [24] Whoever does not love me does not keep my words. And the word that you hear is not mine but the Father's who sent me.

⁵ These things I have spoken to you while I am still with you. ²⁶ But the Helper, the Holy Spirit, whom the Father will send in my name, he will teach you all things and bring to your remembrance all that I have said to you. ²⁷ Peace I leave with you; my peace I give to you. Not as the world gives do I give to you. Let not your hearts be troubled, neither let them be afraid. ²⁸ You heard me say to you, 'I am going away, and I will come to you.' If you loved me, you would have rejoiced, because I am going to the Father, for the Father is greater than I. ²⁹ And now I have told you before it takes place, so that when it does take place you may believe. ³⁰ I will no longer talk much with you, for the ruler of this world is coming. He has no claim on me, ³¹ but I do as the Father has commanded me, so that the world may know that I love the Father. Rise, let us go from here.

Observing the Text

Who is speaking in this passage?

____

____

____

List any words or phrases describing God the Father and his actions in this passage.

____

____

____

How does Jesus demonstrate his love for the Father (verse 31)?

____

____

____

Interpreting the Text

In what ways is God the Father involved in our spiritual growth as believers?

____

____

____

How would you explain the interactions between the members of the Trinity in this passage? Do you see any difference in roles or relationships?

____

____

____

What does it mean when Jesus says, "the Father is greater than I" in verse 28? Make sure to consider this question in light of the understanding that they are both God, perfect in every way and fully possessing all the attributes of deity (along with the Holy Spirit).

____

____

____

Teaching

God speaks primarily through the Bible and through prayer. That's why this study has been focused on those two means of communication. However, there are other ways that God might speak today. It would be wise to approach these ways of hearing God's voice with caution, because we are prone to confuse it with other voices that might influence our thinking. Let's do a quick overview of other ways that God might speak today.

Prophecy

Prophecy today (and in the New Testament) takes on a different meaning than prophecy in the Old Testament. As we discussed previously, prophecy in the Old Testament was spoken and recorded as the inspired word of God. However, as Wayne Grudem notes, a study of prophecy in the New Testament shows us that it could best be defined as "telling something that God has spontaneously brought to mind."[1] Prophecy today is not God's authoritative word. It should be considered merely human words, and therefore not equal in authority to the Bible.[2] Anyone who desires to share a "word" ought to do so with humility and at least be willing to accept that it may not be from God. Rather than saying, "Thus says the Lord," a more appropriate way to speak of prophecy is to say, "I think that the Lord wants me to share with you." Additionally, any prophecy should be tested by Scripture. If it really is from God, then it cannot contradict the authority of the Bible.

Promptings

When you become a follower of Jesus, the Holy Spirit dwells in you. As you walk with God, he leads, illuminates, and teaches you through the inner witness of the Holy Spirit. You might suddenly be reminded of a passage of Scripture that directly applies to a situation in which you find yourself. You might think of a person you haven't thought of in a long time and sense that the Spirit is moving you to pray for that person or contact them. You might have a strong feeling that you're supposed to do something or go somewhere. You might feel like you should give a generous gift to a particular person and in so doing find out that person had been praying that God would provide for a need. These "promptings" take the shape of an inner sense, confirmation, or spontaneous thought. Like prophecy, promptings are not authoritative. They could be wrong and therefore should be tested by Scripture and held onto loosely. Spending regular

---

1 Grudem, *Systematic Theology*, 1050.
2 Ibid., 1055.

time reading the Bible, praying, and engaging in other spiritual disciplines helps to tune our ears to hear the Holy Spirit speak in this way.

People

The Holy Spirit unites the church as one body. The body functions in interdependent relationships where we need one another for wisdom and encouragement. In God's sovereignty, he does not provide individual believers with everything they need within themselves. Instead, he enables people with a beautiful diversity of gifts, personalities, experiences, and passions to be part of a community. This means that God often desires to speak to you through someone else. It may come in the form of encouragement or comfort when gathering for corporate worship. Often when attempting to discern God's will, clarity and confirmation will come through the wise counsel of other mature believers. Therefore, seek the input of those God has placed in your life who can provide godly counsel. These are people who love you enough to tell you the truth even when it's not something you want to hear.

Questions for Reflection

What is the danger in seeing these kind of leadings as having the same authority as the Bible?

____

____

____

Have you ever followed a prompting that you couldn't explain? If so, what happened as a result?

____

____

____

Do you have a regular habit of seeking wisdom from other mature believers when you're making decisions? Why or why not? What could be the benefits of this habit?

____

____

____

Prayer

Thank God for the many ways that he reveals himself to us, continually drawing us deeper into the walk of faith. Pray that his voice would be clear, distinct, and impossible to ignore.

SCRIPTURE MEMORY

When the Spirit of truth comes, he will__________into all the truth, for he____________ on his own author-ity, but whatever he hears he will speak, and he will______________ the things that are to come. —*John 16:13*

FILTERING OUT OTHER VOICES

Scripture Study

John 14:15-31

If you love me, you will keep my commandments. [16] *And I will ask the Father, and he will give you another Helper, to be with you forever,* [17] *even the Spirit of truth, whom the world cannot receive, because it neither sees him nor knows him. You know him, for he dwells with you and will be in you.*

[18] *I will not leave you as orphans; I will come to you.* [19] *Yet a little while and the world will see me no more, but you will see me. Because I live, you also will live.* [20] *In that day you will know that I am in my Father, and you in me, and I in you.* [21] *Whoever has my commandments and keeps them, he it is who loves me. And he who loves me will be loved by my Father, and I will love him and manifest myself to him."* [22] *Judas (not Iscariot) said to him, "Lord, how is it that you will manifest yourself to us, and not to the world?"* [23] *Jesus answered him, "If anyone loves me, he will keep my word, and my Father will love him, and we will come to him and make our home with him.* [24] *Whoever does not love me does not keep my words. And the word that you hear is not mine but the Father's who sent me.*

25 These things I have spoken to you while I am still with you. 26 But the Helper, the Holy Spirit, whom the Father will send in my name, he will teach you all things and bring to your remembrance all that I have said to you. 27 Peace I leave with you; my peace I give to you. Not as the world gives do I give to you. Let not your hearts be troubled, neither let them be afraid. 28 You heard me say to you, 'I am going away, and I will come to you.' If you loved me, you would have rejoiced, because I am going to the Father, for the Father is greater than I. 29 And now I have told you before it takes place, so that when it does take place you may believe. 30 I will no longer talk much with you, for the ruler of this world is coming. He has no claim on me, 31 but I do as the Father has commanded me, so that the world may know that I love the Father. Rise, let us go from here.

Observing the Text

List any words or phrases which Jesus uses to describe himself and his actions in this passage.

____

____

____

How does Jesus say that we demonstrate our love for him (verses 21 and 23)?

____

____

____

In verse 27, what does Jesus give to his disciples? How does he want their hearts to respond to his gift?

____

____

____

Interpreting the Text

In what ways is God the Son involved in our spiritual growth as believers?

____

____

____

Jesus keeps talking about leaving in this passage. What is he talking about? What specific verses lead you to that conclusion?

____

____

____

In verse 29, Jesus says, "And now I have told you before it takes place, so that when it does take place you may believe." What does he want them to believe?

____

____

____

Teaching

At a live music performance, there is a person tasked with balancing, adjusting, and mixing all the sounds called the audio engineer. They are true artists with highly trained ears that enable them to craft an overall sound that is pleasing to the audience. During rehearsals, the audio engineer intently listens for anything that needs to be corrected or adjusted. Every auditorium or concert venue is unique, as soundwaves behave differently depending on the architecture and material used in construction. Audio engineers pick up on sounds that are imperceptible to the average ear like an instrument slightly out of tune or feedback from one of the speakers. Somehow they're able to filter out all the other sounds that fill the room to focus their attention on the one that needs to be heard.

You live your life in a room filled with voices. Yet among all those voices, there is one voice that speaks Truth and Life. The voice of God is the most important voice in the room. As Isaiah 40:8 reminds us, *"The grass withers, the flower fades, but the word of our God will stand forever."* His voice is more powerful than all the voices you will hear in your life. Those voices (including your own) will wither and fade, but God's voice will echo for all eternity. One of the most important disciplines of a follower of Jesus is to train our ears to filter out all the other voices in our lives, so we can focus our attention on the one that needs to be heard above all — the voice of God.

Knowing for certain that you're hearing from God and not just hearing your own voice can be a challenge. Sometimes the answer is not very clear, but there are ways that we can better discern God's will in a particular situation. Ask yourself these questions to help filter out the other voices so you can hear God.

Does this align with Scripture?

To hear God, immerse yourself in the Bible. Read it, study it, and memorize it so that you can know if something you think God is saying aligns with something he's already said. This is the most important filter when trying to discern God's will.

Does this align with what I know about the character of God?

Just as God will not say something that contradicts his word, he will not say something that contradicts his character. He will not tell you to be evil or harsh. He will not tell you to be selfish or greedy. As you read the Bible and spend time praying, seek to know God's character.

Does this seem wise?

If you sense that God is leading you in a particular direction, use your common sense. God is probably not telling you to open a snowboard rental shop in the Bahamas. We should note, common sense is not our ultimate authority. It's not beyond the character of God to call his people to act by faith in ways that seem foolish to the world. We can only imagine what people thought of Noah for building a giant ark on dry land. Likewise, God might be calling you to do something that requires extraordinary faith. However, it's best to evaluate the wisdom of a decision against your common sense.

Does this serve or make much of me?

Check your motivations. We can easily mistake God's voice for our own. Since God's ultimate aim is to glorify himself, we should be cautious when we think he's telling us to do something that would bring glory to ourselves. That doesn't necessarily mean God is not leading you in that direction, but it should warn us to pause. We should be wary of things that our hearts perk up to.

Do wise people in my life affirm what I'm hearing?

Fill your life with people who walk with God, seek to hear his voice, and live a life of repentance and faith. Don't ask "yes people." Seek out those who will speak the honest truth to you with grace and love. God will often speak through others to confirm or correct our thinking. Talk to multiple people. They might be able to help you think through passages in the Bible that speak to your situation. They may have an experience that God brought them through, and now he intends to use their gained wisdom in your life.

Asking these questions might not give you perfect clarity, but they will help you evaluate what you sense God is saying. The goal is to filter out the other voices in your head so you can listen to and obey the voice of God above all.

Questions for Reflection

In what ways can studying the Bible "tune our ears" to hear God's voice in other ways? How have you experienced this?

____

____

____

Have you ever followed a leading that you thought was from God at the time, but looking back, you are pretty sure that it wasn't his voice? Which of these questions might have helped you to more clearly identify his guidance?

____

____

____

Who are the mature Christians who you seek out for wise counsel? If you don't have anyone like this in your life, where could you find them? What kind of vulnerability would this require of you?

____

____

____

Prayer

Praise God the Spirit, who promises to lead us into all truth. Pray that his voice would be unmistakable to your ears and that he would give you the faith to follow where he leads.

SCRIPTURE MEMORY

__________________of truth comes, he will guide you into____________, for he will not speak on his own authority, but whatever he hears he will speak, and he will declare to you the _______________________. *—John 16:13*

GOD TOLD YOU WHAT?!

Scripture Study

John 14:15-31

If you love me, you will keep my commandments. [16] And I will ask the Father, and he will give you another Helper, to be with you forever, [17] even the Spirit of truth, whom the world cannot receive, because it neither sees him nor knows him. You know him, for he dwells with you and will be in you.

[18] I will not leave you as orphans; I will come to you. [19] Yet a little while and the world will see me no more, but you will see me. Because I live, you also will live. [20] In that day you will know that I am in my Father, and you in me, and I in you. [21] Whoever has my commandments and keeps them, he it is who loves me. And he who loves me will be loved by my Father, and I will love him and manifest myself to him." [22] Judas (not Iscariot) said to him, "Lord, how is it that you will manifest yourself to us, and not to the world?" [23] Jesus answered him, "If anyone loves me, he will keep my word, and my Father will love him, and we will come to him and make our home with him. [24] Whoever does not love me does not keep my words. And the word that you hear is not mine but the Father's who sent me.

[25] These things I have spoken to you while I am still with you. [26] But the Helper, the Holy Spirit, whom the Father will send in my name, he will teach you all things and bring to your remembrance all that I have said to you. [27] Peace I leave with you; my peace I give to you. Not as the world gives do I give to you. Let not your hearts be troubled, neither let them be afraid. [28] You heard me say to you, 'I am going away, and I will come to you.' If you loved me, you would have rejoiced, because I am going to the Father, for the Father is greater than I. [29] And now I have told you before it takes place, so that when it does take place you may believe. [30] I will no longer talk much with you, for the ruler of this world is coming. He has no claim on me, [31] but I do as the Father has commanded me, so that the world may know that I love the Father. Rise, let us go from here.

Observing the Text

List any words or phrases describing God the Spirit and his actions in this passage.

____

____

____

Who knows the Spirit? Who doesn't (verse 17)?

____

____

____

Who sends the Spirit (verse 26)?

____

____

____

Interpreting the Text

In what ways is God the Spirit involved in our spiritual growth as believers?

____

____

____

Why is it significant that the Spirit will be both with us and in us?

____

____

____

Why do you think Jesus calls him "the Spirit of Truth" in verse 17? In what ways is truth his defining characteristic?

____

____

____

Teaching

In college, I (Ryan) had a female friend who went on a coffee date with a guy from her chemistry class. While she sipped on her latte, he looked into her eyes and said, "God told me we're going to get married." She sat speechless, not sure how to respond, and instantly regretted accepting his invitation to the date. After an awkward long pause, she took a breath, confidently leaned forward, and said, "Well, God hasn't told me that, and until he does, this is going to be our only date." They didn't get married.

We conclude this study with some helpful tips on how to talk about hearing God's voice. God's voice is heard most clearly in the pages of Scripture. Outside of accurately interpreting the Bible, our ability to hear God's voice is subject to being mistaken for things we might desire. Therefore, we hold loosely the things we think we might have heard from God. No matter how confident we might be, if we cannot give a chapter and verse of the Bible for what we think God had said to us, we should hesitate to speak so definitively. As we discussed previously, we should have a healthy skepticism towards ourselves and acknowledge the tendency of our hearts to deceive us.

The way that we talk about hearing God's voice should reflect this humble posture. We stand confidently on God's word, knowing it is without error and will always be fulfilled. But we know that what does not explicitly appear in the Bible could be subject to our desires for ourselves, rather than what God has truly revealed.

By saying, "God told me…" or "God said to me…" we are making a dangerously confident claim. We are saying that what follows is the authoritative word of God. Again, if you're about to quote Scripture, then that's a perfectly appropriately way to start. However, if you're about to say something that was "put on your heart," then you should leave a little more room in your statement to be mistaken. We're human so we often are.

A more appropriate way to talk about hearing God's voice might be to say,

> "I *feel* like God wants me to encourage you by saying…"
> "It *seems* like God is leading…"
> "I *think* God is saying…"

These minor changes don't reflect a lack of confidence in God but in ourselves. In this way, we express our dependence on him and his ability to confirm (or correct) what we think he's saying to us.

Questions for Reflection

Have you ever heard someone claim that God had revealed something to them, but it turned out not to be true or helpful? What are the dangers in this kind of claim?

____

____

____

What does it look like when we speak into the lives of others with humility? How might that affect how our words are received?

____

____

____

How has this study impacted how you hear God's voice? What new habits do you need to establish? How can your group hold you accountable to make lasting changes as a result of the past 12 weeks?

____

____

____

Prayer

Praise the Son of God who humbled himself to become human and dwell with us, giving us both new life and an example to follow. Pray that we would willingly humble ourselves in our words, our attitudes, and our actions. Thank God that he hasn't left us alone in the darkness, but instead chose to speak words of light to guide us each day.

WEEKLY EXERCISE

HEARING GOD'S VOICE

We live in a noisy and busy world. It seems as though there is little time for solitude unless we intentionally make the time. For this exercise, spend 30 minutes in prayer and be prepared to share about it with your group. Find a quiet place where you won't be distracted or interrupted. Be sure to turn off your phone. Start by quieting your mind and asking God to speak. Think through the Model Prayer or one of your memory verses. Let the Spirit direct your prayer.

Get Ready for Group

Write your memorized Scripture.

____

____

____

____

What observations and interpretations of Scripture were most meaningful to you?

____

____

____

____

Summarize your key takeaway(s) for this week.

____

____

____

____

What will you tell the group about the results of your exercise this week?

____

____

____

____

How has this week helped you better understand and apply the Spiritual Growth Grid?

____

____

____

____

____

Made in the USA
Monee, IL
08 July 2026

56723842R00184